Straight from the
horse's
heart

A Spiritual Ride through Love, Loss and Hope

R.T. Fitch

Photography by Terry Fitch

ISBN: 1-4392-1428-X
ISBN-13: 9781439214282
Library of Congress Control Number: 2008909404

Visit www.forceofthehorse.com to order additional copies.

"In the spirit of Dian Fossey, R.T. Fitch touches on a highly emotional and controversial subject in a way that few have dared. When the masses share his commitment to personally shoulder the responsibility of animal welfare, the horse will be in a much better place."

Ky Mortensen – Author of *Horses of the Storm*

...one humid Nigerian evening, I walked across the street into the tall grass again. I was hoping to find a clue; to catch a feeling; to sense her presence, but she was gone. The tropical breeze caused the tall reed grass to rustle and the palms to dance; yet, she was nowhere to be seen. I closed my eyes, took a deep breath, and called to her from deep within me... all was quiet; but, my memories were still intact and I could see her standing before me, enjoying my touch, munching on the fruit, and sharing her story. The vision caused me to smile...and to remember my promise. 'I will tell them your story,' I had said, and she had asked 'Why?' 'Because, maybe it will touch someone who can make a difference; all it takes is one.'
—an excerpt from *His Eyes Upon Me*

A horse listener at heart, in *Straight from the Horse's Heart: A Spiritual Ride through Love, Loss, and Hope*, R.T. Fitch reaches deep into himself and the heart of the horse to carve out the thirty emotionally charged vignettes of this collection.

Touching the hearts of horse lovers, he also reaches into the quarry of men and women who have never experienced the joy of gazing into the eyes of an equine friend. Truly, hasn't each of us asked for a pony at some point as a child? Haven't most of us been entranced by the fluid, elegant beauty of an equine Olympic competitor? Horses inspire us, their loyalty charms us, their diligence, and raw power enchants us.

Saddle up; you are in for a journey of the heart.

This book is dedicated to the memories of:

My Mother
Grace Joan Wills Fitch
1931–2004
She always laughed at my jokes, greeted me with a smile and
a hug while teaching me that it was okay for a man to cry.

My Horse
Ethan
1989–2007
My teacher and mentor, who taught me to slow down,
keep quiet, and listen. He was the voice of the herd.

ACKNOWLEDGEMENTS

Terry Z. Fitch (my wife) for her unwavering support and hard work in putting this project together. She now has entirely new definitions for run-on sentences, poor punctuation, and improper syntax. Her love, obviously, knows no bounds.

*

Grace Joan Wills Fitch (my mother) who taught me that it was okay for a man to be in touch with his "softer side."

*

Chris and Gertrude Ziegler for being the most understanding in-laws who walk on the face of this earth.

*

Jerry Finch, president and founder of Habitat for Horses, who has stood alongside of me and encouraged me to write all the way. He is my brother in spirit.

*

Leslie Anne Webb, renowned equine artist, for her support, insight, guidance, and friendship.

*

Habitat for Horses Volunteers Paula Schmidt, Rebecca Williams, Virginia Seeman, Connie Carmichael, Julie Caramante, Charlotte Wendenburg (and many, many more) for their years of close support and friendship.

*

Ethan for touching my soul and forcing the issue.

*

Apache for bringing joy into my wife's life.

*

Harley for always being there as the gentle and wise giant.

*

Bart for teaching me to face my fears.

*

Pele for reminding me that it is okay to never grow up.

*

Niki for loving me to the point of an obsession.

*

Willie Nelson for lending his support to Habitat for Horses.

And, thanks to all those who have ever shared a kind word and worked towards helping the horses. You may not be mentioned, here, but your self-sacrifice and selfless service is annotated in a much larger and grander book.

TABLE OF CONTENTS

PROLOGUE

I. THE BEGINNING

The writing of this simple introduction was one of the more difficult things that I have done. The stories contained within this book were written with great passion, free flowing, and in one sitting. This introduction/explanation is none of the above. I am forced to write, with my brain, and not use my heart; so, I sincerely feel like a fish out of water. However, stepping outside of one's comfort zone can be a good thing, as I hope the experience of reading this book will be for you.

Looking back, I have tried to visualize exactly when that certain something clicked, not only in my brain, but also in my heart and soul. When did I start to ask serious questions about self-actualization and then expand my thinking outwards to others? It has taken some serious cranial cleaning to come up with a specific period in my early years. I believe that the first time I became aware of the fact that we were not the only intelligent and sentient inhabitants upon this planet was when I was in my early twenties. I was a young married man in the military during the end of the Vietnam era. My last duty station was a pretty rough one, but someone had to do it. I was forced to live on the beautiful island of Oahu, within the Pacific Hawaiian Islands, while on active duty with the United

States Air Force. I was in the band. The trauma of that abuse has scared me for life, in more ways than one.

While performing my military duty as a member of the Air Force Band at Hickam AFB, I developed a new hobby or pastime; I became immersed in the sea and all it was—literally. I soon evolved into an avid diver, body surfer, catamaran sailor, and just one all around beach bum. My Air Force buddies and I would load up my VW V-bus with our dive gear before we drove to the base each day. It is difficult to recall if we ever missed a chance to catch a quick dive in one of many mind-bending locations on the way home. I was hooked so badly that I would have rather been diving than doing most other things that young men hold near and dear to their hearts. I connected with the ocean, and all that was below the surface was a brother of mine: no spear fishing, no scavenging; just watching, touching, experiencing, and learning. I was a child, and student, of the sea.

This passion for all that frolicked in salt water drove me to volunteer and donate my weekends at the local Marine Park where whales swam, dolphins jumped, sea lions roared, and penguins squawked. Call me crazy. Money was tight, and I could have been working a part time job and earning a few extra dollars; but, no, I gladly gave it all away for the magic that was the sea.

I was, at first, given all of the nasty chores that a worker at the bottom of the food chain would be expected to perform; but I did them all with great zeal. Be it filling all the feeding buckets with the correct amounts of smelly herring or shoveling penguin poop out of their enclosure, I was there. The fact that I was just "there" amidst the smells, sights, and sounds of all that was the excitement of the sea was enough for me. Even to this day, I have fond memories of those times.

It did not take long for my excitement and commitment to excellence to be noted by the park's head trainer. I had established favorable ties with the other trainers, but did not have the opportunity to chat much with the woman in charge. She was busy working with several well-known scientists at the Dolphin Research Center, just down the beach. In a way, I was very much in awe of her. She was a tall, muscular, blonde, with a Swedish accent, but most of all, knowledgeable. She was one of the leading dolphin experts in the world. I secretly worshiped the ground that she walked upon, but never let it show.

One Saturday, she asked me if I would like to work with the penguins; she would help teach me how they asked the birds to perform their behaviors before an audience. Heck, I jumped right onto that. How difficult could it be? They were already trained! It was simply a matter of a few weeks, and I was the official "Penguin Trainer" during the weekend shows. But, to me, it was only a taste; I wanted more.

So, off we went to the main show in the Whaler's Lagoon where the trainers and actors put on a show about an evil whaling man and how a Hawaiian Princess and her whale save him. As corny as it sounds, it was an effective presentation, as it was designed to show the Japanese tourists just how brutal and senseless whaling was. With that in mind, it did not bother me to play the bad guy with the striped shirt and harpoon in hand. It afforded me the opportunity to work with pilot whales, false killer whales, and dolphins. I thought that I had died and gone to heaven.

I performed other public jobs as well, such as feeding the fish underwater as a diver in the ocean reef tank, working with the sea lions, and acting as the announcer in a pinch. Even so, there was still something missing. I wanted more, but did not know what it was until the lead trainer said, "It's time for you to get into the water with a new dolphin; she will be yours to work with."

I had my own dolphin. She was all mine to work with and train. I could not believe it! With this, a wonderful bittersweet love affair began: Maleeva and me. There is a story in this book on this subject, so I will not go into detail and spoil it for you, except to say, it was she who first opened the door and showed me the other side of the world. She gave me the key to a new dimension. However, it also was what occurred to our relationship that turned me bitter, and caused me to slam and lock that door shut for many decades. My heart turned to stone until...

II. THE AWAKENING

...another female warmed it up and slowly pulled it open again. This female did not swim with fins in the sea. No, this female walked on two legs and became guilty not just of opening up my heart, but also of stealing it, even to this day. Many decades and relationships after losing Maleeva, I met Terry Ziegler.

Terry awakened my heart as no other woman had, and trust me, there were a few other women. I don't know if you would call it love at first sight but it was sure "like" at first sight, almost tipping off the edge to "lust when first seen." (Is that a real saying?) We were both grown adults and managed our issues in a mature fashion, in spite of me. Until only a few months later, on Christmas morning of 1996, I kneeled on bended knee in front of her parents, my parents, and her grandmother, and asked her to be my wife. She whispered, "Yes," while her grandmother called out, "What did he say?" And so, amidst laughs, tears, and a roomful of hope, we all looked to the future and prayed.

In a matter of just a few weeks from our engagement, I was given notice that I was to be transferred to our Brazil office by our employer. The departure date was mid-March and Terry, being an employee of the same company, could not accompany me as "married status" unless we were, uh, er, "married." So, on February 14, 1997 (Valentine's Day), we exchanged vows before a justice of the peace and prepared to begin our life's adventure.

We spent four interesting and fulfilling years in Brazil. While there, Terry finished another college degree through distance learning, and I began studies for another one of my own. I kept very busy while Terry struggled with things to keep herself occupied. We men could go to work, but the expatriate wives had to create activities. One year passed, then two, then three; and by the time we hit the fourth one, Terry had acquired some pretty rock solid friends and was beginning to enjoy her "retirement."

Then, one fateful day, a friend of hers decided that she wanted a horse. Perhaps, working with and caring for a horse would help make the hours and days seem fuller. And, with that, the girls began a quest for horses in the hills of Macaé, Brazil. You know, of course, if one has a horse the others are going to have to go down the same road, as it would not be a "group thing" unless all were involved in the same activity, together.

Hence, the journey of learning about and acquiring a horse in Brazil began in earnest. Looking for a horse in a foreign country was an entirely different project than doing so in good ole Texas, USA. In Brazil, the national breed is called a Mangalarga Marchador, which is a relatively small horse with a very sublime gait that lets one relax in the saddle for hours. So, the hunt was on. During that quest for an equine charge, Terry suffered a very serious crushing injury when she fell off and, ultimately, was stepped on by a horse that she was considering buying. The injury resulted in a flight back to the U.S. for treatment and her absence from Brazil for several months. There were wounds both physical and emotional that had to heal. The doctor would not let her resume horseback riding for six months. Her inner uncertainties were another question, so I set about working on dispelling those fears.

Prior to her accident, she had looked at one little Mangalarga gelding, and the both of them just seemed to click. So, while Terry was still in the U.S. recovering, I purchased the little guy whose name was, and still is, Apache.

It was our experience with horses in Brazil that further began to soften my heart and melt my soul, not that the process is complete, but it began there. In an effort to participate in my wife's interest, I too obtained a horse so that we could ride together. Through that "looking" process, we became very aware that many, many horses were not being treated with compassion, and that there was a very real need for education, rescue, and equine rehabilitation in rural Brazil.

We managed to locate a friend and trail partner for me; but, in that process, we also purchased several horses that were in dire straits, and began to rehabilitate them. That was when it all started; the thought and desire to help horses in need began to grow.

Prior to being called back to the U.S., we began scouring the Web for U.S. based equine rescues in an effort to learn more about tending to the needs of horses that were either abused or neglected. We found many, and sat back for several months and watched how they performed. After some time, two reputable rescues floated to the surface. Lone Star Equine Rescue (LSER) and Habitat for Horses (www.habitatforhorses.org) were the organizations that caught our eye. We lurked in the background, on their forums and email groups, and absorbed as much as we could about helping those who could not help themselves.

Then it happened; the day came when we had to return to the United States. This singular event caused much upheaval in our household as Terry had made a promise to her four-legged soul mate that she would never leave him and she was hell bent on not breaking that promise. After great expense and much agony, we, the cat, the dog, and Terry's horse made it back to Houston, Texas. Regrettably, I could not bring my horse with me, but did make him a present to our Brazilian stable hand who worshipped the ground that the horse walked on. To acquire my horse was like winning the lotto for him, and I was very, very, confident that a good home was found for my friend. Nevertheless, there was still a hole in my heart and, as we progressed, it did not heal.

III. THE CONTACT

Once back in the U.S., we found ourselves in the same predicament that we originally found ourselves while in Brazil: Terry had a horse, and I did not. As you know, it is the obligation of every married man to endeavor to indulge his wife in all that she loves. With this in mind, I began to look for a horse for myself, but with a twist. Instead of buying a horse out of the want ads, we looked at auctions and rescues where horses really, really needed a home. And we found one: a big, gentle, fat Appaloosa named Ethan who was being auctioned for the stable fees that were owed to his past boarding stable. His prior owners just moved off and left him. If he were not sold at this auction, he would be headed off to one of the two slaughterhouses that were still functioning in Texas at that time. We could not let that happen, so we brought him home that Saturday afternoon. Sweet, sweet, Ethan; he was so calm and gentle, until the drugs wore off. The next day that horse tried to kill me more than one time, and, to date, I have never met such an angry, aggressive, and dangerous horse. We were terrified, yet we had made a commitment. Obviously, I was not going to throw a saddle blanket over his back anytime soon.

Instead of shopping for other horses, we decided to "foster" rescued horses. Not only would we be helping the horses, but also we could determine if we bonded. Originally, we were going to join and volunteer at Habitat for Horses, but at that time, the group was ranch-based and it was over an hour away from our property. We would have been of little use, plus we had the property and barn to house horses and work right at our own location. With this in mind, we joined Lone Star Equine Rescue, an Internet-based rescue group that had no facilities but did have an early developing foster network. So, foster we did. Folks, I am here to tell you, we made rotten foster parents. Having adopted most of our "foster children," we soon realized that we were worthless at this endeavor and decided to give to the rescue in other ways. We fell in love with just about every horse that moved into our barn.

In addition to our day jobs, we worked the rescue seven days a week. In fact, the phone for the rescue rang at our house, and Terry became the physical voice of the group. Before you knew it, we were on the board of directors. Most of our spare time slipped through our fingers as our newly adopted family languished in the pasture. We spent more time with other people's horses and issues than we did with our own. It pains me to look back and realize that it got progressively worse instead of better.

One year after returning to the greater Houston area, I accepted a job offer in Louisiana, and the entire family was packed up and moved to Cajun Country. Terry was so excited— we were out of Texas. Being that the rescue was a Texas-based group, she thought that we had a shot at reclaiming our lives; but I wouldn't have it. I insisted that she be the treasurer for the group and all semblance of a normal life quietly swirled down the drain. Once again, our horses stared at us from over the pasture's fence.

After a few months of being ignored and seeing us work to better the state of affairs for their equine brethren, our herd took the matter into their own hands. That is what this book is about: when the herd decided to speak, and I learned to listen.

IV. THE PLAYERS

Being that this collection of stories is about real people and real horses, it might not be a bad idea to take a few seconds and give a little background on these very special and unique individuals.

__Terry Ziegler Fitch__: As you already know, Terry is my bride, my companion, and my best friend. Terry is the stable one in our relationship; she has the common sense and bookkeeping savvy that keeps us alive and moving forward. She is the engineer; I am the dreamer. She is the one who prompted me to publish these stories since they moved her, and if the engineer is touched by a tale, most normal people are sure to be.

Terry does not know what I am about to write and I know that she will see it upon editing. I have gained so much respect for her during her efforts and work with the rescue organization. Terry proved to be an outstanding, treasurer, organizer, and mediator. She was the "good" officer who could calm people down and make everything right. Terry single-handedly held the organization together when we merged Habitat for Horses and LSER. It was a painful process, and she rose to the occasion to do the "right thing."

Before Hurricane Katrina struck Louisiana, Terry had already logged our names, contact information, and property with LSU and the state's veterinary service as an emergency refuge in case of a natural disaster. Whom do you think they called after Katrina? Terry.

Our organization responded to that disaster. I never expected Terry to slosh through the mud and water to save stranded horses, but she was right there. She also helped to manage the donations of goods and supplies that were coming into Habitat for Horses in Texas and then shipped over to Louisiana for distribution. She did an outstanding job; so much so, that when Rita struck and took all of our shingles away, I received a phone call from LSU's veterinary school and we mutually decided that Terry should help manage the local animal rescue and recovery facility for the four-legged victims of Rita. And again, she was there. In fact, she was still there working months after Rita was a dark and dim memory. She was there ensuring that the last animal was placed with their rightful family; and they were. She shined like she had never shone before, and I love her for every second of it.

Jerry Finch: I almost don't know where to begin when it comes to talking about Jerry. Few people who walk this earth are like this man. Perhaps the jury is still out as to whether that is a good thing or a bad thing. But, this I can say and confirm in print: I have rarely, if ever, said, "I love you" to another man, but I can speak those words to Jerry for I love him like a brother.

If there was a law requiring that you had to list an individual's ingredients on the underside of their right forearm, his would read something like this:

20% Magic

15% Nurturing Mother

10% Salesman

5% Politician

50% BS

And I mean that…fifty percent BS in terms of not only being able to dish it out, but also the ability to take it in return. You just cannot take yourself too seriously if your one and only 24/7 activity for the past ten years has been exclusively horse rescue. You need to have pretty thick skin if you hope to survive; and Jerry flourishes.

Jerry is the illustrious Founder and President of Habitat for Horses. He is not only the blood and guts of the group, but he is the heart that pumps the life into every human and horse that meets him. Making sure that a horse does not suffer is Jerry's passion in life, and his fire has lit the candle of many people across the globe, including mine.

It was several years ago when Jerry Finch sat across a table from me while we calmly sipped on ice-cold beer and told me that I should write. He said that I should commit to paper what I had experienced with my mother's death and how it not only affected me, but how the power of the horses ran through that entire period in time. He said that others would take heart from hearing such a story; so, I wrote. The tale in question is the second story in this collection.

To have Jerry Finch tell me to write was a great honor as Jerry is an astoundingly profuse and passionate writer himself. He moves me and those who know him; I could not let him down.

I owe a lot to Jerry and hope that we can grow old, or older, together as I just can't imagine a world without my "Older Brother" in it; nor can many other people and horses, alike. Thanks Jerry.

Leslie Anne Webb: If you have been around horses for any length of time, you most certainly have run across the name and work of equine artist Leslie Anne Webb. Leslie's work speaks to the spirit of those she paints. If you want an original oil painting that looks like a photograph of your horse, don't call Leslie. But if you would like to see the soul and spirit of your equine partner jump right off the canvas and wrap its legs around you, email Leslie—she's the one you want. Back before the Christmas of '03, I needed a very special Christmas present for Terry. Heck, I had given her Apache as a Christmas present several years earlier; how could I top that? So, how about an original oil painting of her horse, commissioned by a famous artist, to have and to hold until death do they part, and beyond? Great idea! I just needed to locate the right artist. With the help of the Internet, I located Leslie (www.lawebb.com).

At first, our communications were emails about Apache and his personality. I forwarded a photo, and we chatted. As the emails bounced back and forth, I began to learn that Leslie had several personal rescue horses of her own. They were more than just pasture ornaments; they were her very best friends. Then the door opened a little more; in fact, I was somewhat shocked that this special woman would begin to share some deep and inner secrets with me when it came to the issue of understanding her equine friends. You see, Leslie has the intuitive ability to "sense" or "feel" what it is her horse's are expressing. She began to teach me how to turn off my mind and tune into what was going on around me.

If you ever want to stop a conversation at a social function, just start heading down this road and watch how many people drop out and turn away. For that reason, I proceed cautiously, but this is what the book is about, primarily. Leslie, over several months, taught me to listen for what most humans cannot hear. Once that process began to develop, she then helped me to project what I felt to those to whom I had been listening. Heavy stuff, but you will read more as you go through this book. The stories all are true, but you can be the one to determine just how true they are for you.

I am glad to say that we are still in touch with Leslie and, in fact, had the opportunity to go meet and stay at her ranch in California in the fall of '07. There is a story included in this book regarding that visit. Leslie is a magical and beautiful woman. The land and creatures that surround her radiate that same goodness and love. The way that a brother would feel towards a sister is how to best describe the love in my heart for what Leslie has done, what she now does, and what she intends to do in the future. She will forever be in our hearts.

The Horses

Ethan: Our first U.S. private rescue. He was the meanest, most cantankerous horse that ever walked this planet. He was a horse that we showered with love year after year; the horse that became the Speaker of the Herd; the horse whose cold heart and frozen soul melted when he decided to make me his trail partner; and the best friend that I ever had. Ethan was not only the voice of the herd, but also the leader of the group, although it was difficult to ascertain. His right hand man, Harley, would do most of the dirty work for him while Ethan would stand back and observe. The two of them were an interesting team.

Ethan is the spirit that guides my soul.

Apache: The Brazilian Mangalarga Marchador and the equine soul mate of my wife. I often refer to Apache as the "World's Most Expensive $500 Horse." That was what we paid for him in Brazil, and then we turned around and spent a small fortune to bring him back home to the U.S. As you will find out, a man in love will do anything for the woman who holds his heart.

Apache Stone, meaning hard or tough Indian in Brazil, was most likely a cart horse before we found him. Due to his detached and standoffish manner, we know that he had been beaten and treated with little regard. Although Apache comes off as an aloof grouchy old man, it is only because he does not want you to know that he cares. As you walk into the pasture and the other horses crowd around you for attention, Apache stands far off, but he always watches. Should you ignore him and walk about, he very secretly grazes his way up to you and pretends to act surprised when he picks up his head right at about the level of your hand for a friendly pat. He does not want to appear weak by caring, but he cares and he loves "his" Terry. That is all that matters to me as he brings great joy into my wife's life—and vice versa.

Harley: AKA Ginerous Legacy whose father, Go for Gin, won the 1994 Kentucky Derby. Harley was named after the motorcycle that my wife will never let me own. While training to run in his father's hoof steps, a tragedy befell him and he suffered a slab fracture to his right knee. He was only two years old. Harley's trainer insisted on sending him off to slaughter, but, by the grace of God, the owner stepped in and wanted Harley to have a chance at life. LSER was contacted, and, due to our facilities, the rescue group asked us if we could foster Harley and keep him stalled until his knee healed, if it ever would.

We jumped at the opportunity. So, rescue horse number three graced our property. Harley was so hyped up on steroids and drugs that he literally tore apart the first stall in which we put him. As a result, we were forced to "Harley proof" another stall with steel reinforcement so that he would not kick it to pieces. He was so pumped up and so full of Lord knows what that he almost destroyed his hooves as he kicked and jumped during those first several days. Finally, his system cleared and he settled down to the routine of being in a stall while his knee healed, which it finally did.

Harley presents an interesting story and is quite famous as the mascot of the rescue, prize winner of one of Terry's photos, and an unsolicited subject of one of Leslie Anne Webb's paintings. His story is of such interest and resolve, that a children's book on "Harley, the Rescue Horse," is currently in production. Stay tuned.

<u>Bart</u>: Bart and his brother, Star, were the next additions to the herd. These two Thoroughbreds were born and bred to race, but when the owner decided to pack up and move to another state, Bart and Star would not load so they had to leave them behind. Both of these colts were born in that pasture and had never been out of it. So, when they were asked to leave, they took the easy way out and said "no." That is, until we arrived.

In the heat of a southeast Texas July afternoon, a cowboy buddy and I haltered up these two geldings and decided to walk them to our house some six miles away. The journey is a story to tell in its own right, but we made it. Star was adopted out, while we decided to keep Bart and turn him into my riding horse. Remember, Ethan was unrideable; Harley had the broken knee, which had over-calcified; and Bart might have been green, but he had potential.

So, Bart and I set forth on a journey through trainers, including Linda Parelli. Many broken bones later, we still, today, are not riding. Ole Bart is afraid of just about everything, so it is our quest to build up his self-esteem and confidence. My only hope is that I live long enough to see the biggest horse in the pasture *act* like the biggest horse in the pasture. Only time will tell.

<u>Pele</u>: I smile when I see that name. Little Pele was a red Mustang/Quarter Horse gelding mix that we agreed to foster,

while living in Louisiana. At that time, the bulk of our members and interested adopters lived in Texas, so we had a great deal of trouble getting little Pele adopted. He was such a curious and intelligent little guy, that I really hated to see him leave. Then, a vet diagnosed Apache with COPD, and we felt that Pele might be a good suitor to relieve Apache of his riding duties. So, being the rotten foster parents that we were, we adopted him, too.

As luck would have it, Apache was fine, and Pele had a year or two of being the wise guy of the herd. He so wants to be the boss, but the elder horses will not allow it. I am sure that one day he will wear the crown of the herd, but for the time being, he is still the "little guy."

<u>Niki</u>: Niki was a plush, black and tan, female German Shepherd that we raised from a pup while living in Brazil. If owning horses in a foreign land was not enough, we added a dog to the list, along with Terry's cat, Blizzard, whom we had brought from the States.

We loved Niki and she loved us; but, to this day, we feel that we took her from her mother sooner than she should have been separated. Even as an adult, she was urgent, possessive—almost to the point of being neurotic. She could not rest, she could not sleep, and she could not let us out of her sight. She was almost tiring to be around; but we loved her with all our heart and she loved us.

Niki thought that her job was to protect us from the horses—imagine that. Whenever we were in the pasture, there was Niki, pacing at the fence line watching every move that the horses made. Heaven help us if the horses decided to run. Niki would bark and run up and down the fence line regardless of whether it was day or night. If we tried to work with the horses or get up on one, oh my goodness, there was hell to pay.

Niki was the first puppy I had ever raised in my life. I think there was a bit of my blood running through her veins, as I am about as hyper as she was. I considered her my daughter.

<u>Kenny</u>: We adopted Kenny shortly after we returned to the United States as a companion for Niki. Kenny is a big, loving, goofy, white German Shepherd, and is exactly 180 degrees different from Niki. Sadly, he never managed to slow her down. All she did was shove her ball in his face and attempt to force him to play. Even though she drove him nuts, too, he loved her.

V. THE DOORWAY

Now, you have a little bit of background and a better understanding of what is awaiting you just a few pages away. In good conscience, I warn you on two different levels:

1.) There are stories within this collection that are not for the faint of heart, nor are they for youngsters. There's laughter and love, but there also is a lot of pain, since during this time period, many horses were suffering greatly from slaughter. The three slaughter plants in the U.S. are no longer slaughtering horses, as they were when these stories were written (stories referring to Kaufman, Texas, as an example). But horses are being trucked across our borders for slaughter in Mexico and Canada. So, one step forward, two steps backward.

2.) Every story is true. To what extent you would like to believe the truth is up to you. As an author, I have the right and the obligation to write things as I observe and/or experience them, and that is what I've done here. So, I would ask that you read with an open mind and accept only what your heart tells you to accept. With a philosophy like that, you can never go wrong.

With all of that said, please remember that the bulk of this book is a combination of life events that occurred in real time from late 2003 to the end of 2007. These stories, for the most part, were prompted by emotionally moving events, and I hope that they move you, as well.

"Ethan, it is so!"

I SIT IN WONDER

It started out as any other Saturday: up before the sun, make coffee, check email, say hello to the dogs, greet the horses, and review the list of projects that needed to be accomplished before the sun set in the evening. However, this Saturday had a few dramatic twists. I needed to be several places at one time during the same time frame, so there would have to be some fancy juggling. The electricians were coming out to wire the new horse barn; at the same time, the farrier was arriving to trim the horses' hooves; plus, we needed to pick up a load of hay before noon. So, it was time to dance.

On the morning of Saturday, February 1, 2003, all of Lafayette Parish, Louisiana, was under a dense fog warning. When I stepped out of the house at sunrise, it was obvious that things might be moving a little slower until the fog lifted.

I immediately was greeted by the pair of happy-go-lucky German Shepherds who are always excited on Saturday morning, as they get to go for a ride in the Big Red Truck to get hay. Oh, what fun! As I gazed out into the pastures, I could not make out the four pampered ponies, since the fog was too thick. I walked out through the back of the barn and none of them could be seen, so the odds were pretty good that they were in the back pasture munching down on their round bale. I stepped out several yards, gave a call, and waited. The mist swirled around me like foam in the surf as I listened intently for rumbling hooves, but the morning maintained its silence.

Unhurriedly, like dolphins slipping through the depths, the phantom shadows of the horses gradually began to materialize before me. One at a time, in order, in line, they calmly walked up to me in formation for their rub on the withers, pat on the chest, and scratch on the belly. Each took their turn at receiving their morning hello, until all four circled me. Together, we walked back to the barn.

At the barn, I stopped and surveyed the new side gates that lay against the wall, waiting to be installed by the part-time ranch hand-me. While Harley gently mouthed my cell phone in an effort to steal it from my belt, I began scratching down a list of hardware that I was going to need to accomplish the gate project. I dropped my pen, which meant Harley hit pay dirt as he quickly grabbed my cell phone and gracefully twirled it above my head by the antenna. A big grin emerged on his face, as this was his favorite game. He managed to accomplish the cunning feat without my interference-Harley one, human zero. I carefully retrieved my phone and bent down to pick up my pen when suddenly I heard a distant pop, bang, or shot. Immediately, I became alert to the fact that I was standing amidst a small herd of horses, in limited visibility, with "scary" noises occurring. Quickly, I looked at the horses and then relaxed, as they did not spook; they were not flustered or even nervous. In fact, they were standing in an alert stance, heads held high, and ears at full extension looking to the north/northwest, he opposite direction from whence the sound had come. I wondered if it was a gunshot. The thought slowly slipped away into LaLa Land as I proceeded with my tabulations. After all, who in their right mind would be hunting in the middle of a fog bank?

I remember concluding my list, walking back into the barn, and turning to gaze at our equine children. They were still there, standing in place. In fact, they were in formation, one in front and three in back, staring ever so intently to the northwest. Their formation reminded me of a delta, a triangle pointing into the direction of their labored glare. I was confused. How could they be so interested in looking in the wrong direction? What were they hearing, what did they think they were seeing, and what was going through their minds, as they appeared to be mesmerized and in a trance?

The sight of them there, standing in the mist looking off into nowhere, disturbed me to the point that I called to them. No one budged. I called again, and the head of the Appaloosa slowly turned in my direction just enough so that one sad eye could look at me. I motioned to him, and he slowly turned around, walked to me with his head lowered, and nuzzled my hand. I scratched his forehead and noticed that his right eye had just formed a tear, one lone solitary tear. I asked if he were sad; I asked if he wanted more food; I asked what the problem was. I only heard a gentle sigh in response. I shrugged it off and went back to work.

I did not know that at the time, to the north of our quiet farm, a comet named Space Shuttle Columbia was passing overhead, a bright meteor carrying the souls of seven courageous and generous human beings home. I did not know. I had no clue that seven souls of my species were headed across the bridge high over head. I did not know. Four horses, however, stood gallantly at attention; four horses looked to the sky; and four horses felt something that I did not.

In reflection, I wonder if I did not miss something else that morning, something that my single-minded human brain did not hear, something special, something wondrous. Yet, I was not listening. I now sit in wonder and roll it over in my head time and time again, that gentle sigh, that horsy response, and the tear in that eye. What did it say; what did it mean?

Did I really hear something in the gentle escape of air from those equine lips, a sound so profound that it did not compute at the time it happened?

Was that a gentle whisper, a thought, a suggestion?

Was my soul, and not my ears, hearing those quiet words?

Was the meaning really what I now believe it to be?

Was my heart touched by the souls of the four horses when I still failed to understand? Yet, admittedly, I heard the whisper, the soft voice that spoke on another level. "We are so sorry; we are so very, very sorry."

I sit in wonder.

THE FORCE OF THE HORSE

In early May 2004, I was blessed with the opportunity to sit with Jerry Finch, the founder of Habitat for Horses and one of the few fellow males that I respect on this planet. We shared not only several drinks, but also many words, comments, and thoughts. Jerry is my brother in spirit when it comes to battling the issues of horse slaughter, abuse, and neglect. While we talked, I began to attempt to articulate the feelings and emotions I experienced with the recent passing of my mother and the role that horses played in my life, both at that time and evermore. He lovingly urged me to put to paper those thoughts and expressions before they slipped away, never again to be recovered. So, here I sit, fumbling with a memory that really does not want to cooperate, sort of a self-defense response I would imagine.

My lovely bride, Terry, is the sole human responsible for leading horses into my heart. I never had a desire, care, or an inkling of any interest surrounding involvement with horses. I once was in love with a motorcycle. I used to talk to it, wax it, shine it, and go out and tell it goodnight. But a horse? Never! Horses found their way to me because they were a wish, a desire, and a lifetime dream of my wife's. Any spouse worth their salt would aspire to give their mate their dream; and with that, my wife received her very first horse, Apache. That entire process is a story in itself—probably more dramatic than the few words I plan to share here. But I needed to make the point that horses came to me later in life as an acquired taste and with a conscious effort. So with that said, let me begin.

As I mentioned, Terry received Apache as a Christmas gift several years ago. That singular event has made every other Christmas to follow rather anticlimactic when it comes to Santa and his presents. Last Christmas, I attempted to parallel the event with something special, precious, and lasting. I contacted the world-renowned equine artist, Leslie Anne Webb, and commissioned her to do a portrait of Apache especially for Terry. Now, while in the process of arranging for this piece of art to be created, I learned that Ms. Webb is a gifted and blessed individual who feels the equine spirit on an intuitive level. "Horse-pucky," all we educated-types say. "Can't be...full of nonsense," etc. But, I listened to Ms. Webb, and listened closely. As we communicated and worked out the details (doing a painting does not take days or weeks, it takes months), I began to notice something rather strange, yet beautiful, happening in my own life. So, I decided to test it.

I shared with Ms. Webb that my wife thinks I am nuts. Nonetheless, I had been observing a peculiar behavior in our herd that I did not understand or believe. Our farm, which consists of our home, our barn, and several other buildings, is surrounded completely by our pastures, with the exception of the front yard. The closest pasture to the house is on the western side. In fact, the entire west elevation of the house is committed to our master suite. One of the windows, which looks out over the west pasture, is only a few feet from my side of the bed. The windows have a reflective coating that makes it virtually impossible to see in from the outside, during daylight hours. At 5:00 a.m., when I gaze out that dark window, by the glow of one of our barnyard lights I can see the horses lying in the west pasture, close to the fence, therefore, close to the house. They have many locations from which to choose to sleep, including a nice covered area with beach sand behind the barn, but for some unknown reason they seem to prefer to sleep near us. The sight of those relaxed beings always sets the tone for the day; they focus and center me. But, one thing they do unsettles me. As I stand and stare through that darkened window, I can feel their calmness wash over me; and, as their peace settles my soul, at least one, if not more, turns and looks directly at me. First, the head turns; then, the neck bends, and finally, the gentle eyes calmly stare right through the black glass and touch my soul. It is an unnerving and eerie feeling; yet, somewhere tucked in amongst all that confusion is a foundation of reassurance that they are there for us and want to be no place else. Words fail in describing this feeling.

I shared these occurrences with Ms. Webb via email. She encouraged me to talk to the horses during these times, to utter their names, to express our love. I shared this with Terry.

Again, she thought I was nuts, since she is the engineer in the family and pure business is her forte. I, on the other hand, am a degreed and certified "people person," so abstract is my middle name, as nothing conforms to known formulas. We make a great team and keep each other in balance. Nonetheless, I followed Ms. Webb's advice. The next time I awoke and found the horses sleeping next to us, I uttered in my mind, *Good morning, Harley*, and, without hesitation, that great big Thoroughbred head turned and looked at me as quickly as if I had just shot off a gun. I was speechless; I was shocked; and I headed off to the porcelain-thinking chair to ponder this revelation.

As I continued to work this issue, I tried new variances, and with each one, another revelation. (Mysteriously enough, this works only in the cool, calm, quiet of the early morning.) First, I mentioned each one's name, and they turned and looked, right on cue, as if I were standing out amongst them in the pasture. Then, if they were not close to the fence, I called them. They came and stood, looking over the fence directly at the window. I praised them and told them my thoughts. While, to date, I cannot hear them, I know they hear me. Unfortunately, my mother's health suddenly took a tragic downturn, so I traveled to Florida and left my wife and four-legged family behind.

My mother was the glue that held our family together. If ever I wanted to test out a new joke or comedy line, I tried it on her. It was always a joy to speak with her, as she laughed at everything I said. We were losing her, and her life's light was beginning to dim. I spent a week at her hospital bedside and watched her life ebb away like air out of a balloon, and I could do nothing to stop it. All I could do was be there, lend support, ease the pain, and wait. She was closest to alertness in the early morning. As a result, I would make a point of parking "Big Red," my Dodge dually, where she could see it from her bed next to the window. She liked to look out at it and see the big, aggressive "Fire Pony" painted on the side. She said it looked strong, and in looking strong, it gave her strength. We spoke of family, the past, what was, and what should have been. We had talks about Terry, her "newly acquired" daughter; our home; our animals; and especially, our horses. I am loaded with horse stories, so it was a time to share, make her smile, and give her pleasure and peace. Each day our talks grew shorter; each day she drifted further away; until one day, she stopped talking. So I continued, alone, hoping that she could hear.

The last day that I was there, a horse trailer pulled up out front while I was going to Big Red to use the phone. Two women stepped out of the truck and waved at me as they had seen the Fire Pony on the truck. Curious about their intentions, I walked over and asked what they were doing. They replied that they brought over a Mini (miniature horse) and were taking it into the rehab center's activity area for the more mobile residents to see. (I just moved Mom out of the hospital and into a rehab center where she could rest more comfortably.) I asked the women if they would mind stopping by my mother's room on the way, since she had never seen or met her grand-horses in person and she was quickly fading away on us.

Would they stop in? Heck, they made a huge production out of it, and the strangest thing occurred. My mother, who had not been lucid in days, came alive. They brought the little Mini in, and he hung his head over my mother's bed. She reached up, wrapped her arms around his neck, and did not let go. She whispered, "Hey baby, nice baby," and gently rocked the little Mini who was tenderly nuzzling his muzzle against her neck. I was shocked, touched, and speechless; so was everyone else. All of a sudden, she released her arms, fell back on the bed, and I gently brushed a tear from her cheek. Once the Mini and his crew left, I leaned over to take my mother's hand, and I whispered, "All our horses love you, Mom." Though she did not open her eyes, she gently squeezed my hand.

That sight moved me to the point of going to a nearby store where I purchased a little stuffed horse that looked just like our Harley, the 1,200 lb. equine dog that thinks he should be let inside the house. My mother adored the little stuffed cat that Terry gave her, which she named "Kitty-Kitty," so I brought her another stuffed critter to keep her company. This one was named "Harley." I returned to her room, gave her Harley, and told her that I had to leave and asked if she were okay with that. To my surprise, she said without opening her eyes, "You go home to Terry, tell her I love her. I will be okay because I have Harley and Kitty-Kitty here cheering for me. They will watch over me." Those were the last words I ever heard her say.

The following week, I received a call in the middle of the night from my younger sister. She informed me that the attending nurse just phoned and Mom's time was short. She was heading to the center to be with her and that I should await her call. As I stood up in the darkness and looked out the window, the horses were there. Harley was looking straight at me and I had nothing to say to him. I knew not what to say or think, so I headed for my office and place of work to occupy my mind.

Sitting behind my desk, it did not take me long to realize that I was in the wrong place to take that fateful call. My mind was not on the job, and I was unclear as to what my reaction and outward behavior would be when the call came in. I did not want to be seen by my staff during that period, so I quietly excused myself to go home and surround myself with the love and positive energy that Terry and our animals have built into our farm. Even though Terry was out on business, I felt her strength and presence at home. I gazed out the bedroom window. It was noon, and I could see the horses grazing. As I watched, I felt tired; I stretched out on the bed and fell asleep.

The shrill sound of the phone woke me. I jumped to my feet and looked at the clock; I had been asleep for an hour. The caller ID indicated it was my sister. I looked out the window and saw Harley looking back at me as he gently pressed his massive chest against the fence; his eyes were sad, and there was pain in his expression. As I answered the phone, I heard the words, "She has passed," float out of the earpiece. I paused again and I looked at Harley. He hung his head down over the fence and shook it. I answered, "I know," and Harley sadly walked away. "She passed holding Harley in her arms," said my sister. Again, I choked out, "I know," and hung up.

Today, two Harleys greet the start of my day: one outside wanting to come in, and one little stuffed Harley, my mother's "Harley," which is placed with love in our bedroom so that I can be reminded, everyday and always of the *force of the horse.*

THE FORCE OF THE HORSE CONTINUES

It had been an outstanding weekend, making it difficult to believe that just several hundred miles away hurricane Jeanne was raining terror down on family and friends in Florida. The weather in southern Louisiana was crisp and clear with a gentle north wind blowing. It was Sunday evening, the twenty-sixth day of September 2004, a great day to be outside working with the horses and gardening.

I just finished barbecuing a spicy and delectable dinner for Terry and myself. Afterwards, while the sun peacefully slipped behind the trees to the west, I went to the barn to clean up from feeding the equine children their dinner. Although I didn't barbecue for them, their dinner of feed pellets and rice bran seemed to hit the spot, nonetheless.

I stood silently at the back door of the barn, watching the pasture dolphins leisurely slip off into the darkness of the back pasture, when I heard the unsettling screech of tires. Way back behind our property, on down the ridge, runs a dark county road. With a fleeting glimpse, I could make out a set of taillights moving to the east, slowly turning and skidding sidewise so that I could see both lights aimed directly toward me. The screeching of rubber on asphalt continued for a few moments, and, as the taillights came to an abrupt and rocking halt, I heard a crash, the breaking of glass, and a blood-curdling scream.

For a split second, I stood frozen while my brain attempted to digest the input that it had just received as well as formulate an appropriate response. For that one second, there was silence; then, from far off across the fields, I heard a little child sobbing.

I was off in a flash. I bolted to the house, grabbed my wallet and cell phone, jumped into Big Red the Rescue Truck, and screamed down our driveway in a cloud of burning rubber and diesel exhaust. My exit was so fast that I never notified Terry nor did I know where she was. The old EMT in me had just been activated and the adrenalin was pumping.

Big Red and I flew around the perimeter of our property and soon landed on the road behind us. I could see a single headlight of a vehicle, as it was parked sideways in the road. As I roared up to the scene, I was both surprised and mildly relieved at what Big Red's lights brought into view. The vehicle in question was a mid-sized SUV with a severely damaged right front fender and grill. A woman and small girl stood in front of the vehicle; they were holding each other and crying. Both had their tearful eyes affixed to the crumpled creature that lay in the road before them—a little black calf.

I swiftly stepped out of Big Red with my giant Maglite ablaze and immediately asked if they were injured. Once they acknowledged that they were okay, I queried them on the collision, asking if they had bumped their heads, twisted their necks, etc. The woman stated that both had been wearing their seat belts, but they were concerned for the little calf. With that, I diverted my attention to the baby cow that was sprawled out on the pavement in a position that indicated grievous injury. I put my hand over the moist nose to feel for breath—nothing. I palpated the major artery in the neck and could not locate a pulse. Its eyes were frozen open in a glassy stare, and there was no reaction to light stimulus; the lifeless little creature was gone.

As I knelt on the ground, I spun around at eye level to the sobbing little girl and reassured her that the baby calf was no longer with us. It had crossed over a bridge and was now on the other side. Everything would be okay. The little human girl wanted to take blame, but I assured her there was none; a black calf on a dark country road was invisible to her mother's eyes. It was, is, and will forever be remembered as an accident. I then asked the mother to take the little girl around to the other side of the truck so that she could not see me, unceremoniously drag the dead calf off from the road onto the shoulder. As respectful as I might have intended to be, one man trying to move a 300 plus lb. baby cow is not a pretty picture.

With that done, I fired up the cell phone, made some calls, located the farmer who owns the cows, and expressed my concern as to a possible hole in the fencing and the probability of a reoccurrence of this incident. The woman's husband appeared on the scene; we exchanged vitals, checked the right front end of the SUV for drivability, and then went our separate ways in an effort to recover what was left of a formerly fine day.

I arrived back at our farm to find Terry playing with the horses while gazing eagerly off over the back fence. She had been watching intently across the fields with great concern. I explained to her, with much remorse, what had happened. Sadly, we both shook our heads as I had noticed that particular little calf lying by itself earlier in the day. Not only did it seem unusual to me, but also it apparently concerned the donkey that guards the herd as she had been standing solitary guard over the little calf. At the time, I walked across our pasture to get a better view since so many calves were lost to coyotes last spring. When I approached the fence line, the little rascal jumped up and ran away. I remembered it by the big white blaze across its face.

Terry and I said good night to the horses, petted the German Shepherds, shut the barn doors, and then strolled to the house, hand-in-hand. I opened the back door of the house for Terry to enter, and as I stepped inside, I fell into an abyss that I have yet to climb out of completely. Every phone was ringing, lights were blinking on answering machines, and computer screens were flashing instant messages: something was wrong, bad wrong!

While we were out living a normal country life, someone else's was in peril. One of my sisters called and left an urgent phone message, and then my uncle called. There was a family emergency, and I needed to call them immediately. I looked somberly to Terry with questions in my eyes. She shrugged and said, "You need to call."

I first called my uncle whose number was last on the caller ID; both he and my aunt got onto the line and stressed that I needed to call my sister. There was some problem with my father, and she had all of the information. They were supportive, but their level of concern alarmed me. *My father, what could be wrong with my father?* I was aware that the eye of the storm was just about directly over his home in Citrus Springs, Florida, but it had weakened and should not be a serious threat; besides, my brother and his wife live only a few miles away. *What could possibly be wrong?*

As I dialed my sister's number, I rolled over in my mind what could be wrong. *Surely, there were no health issues, as Dad had just turned seventy- five and his doctor told him that he has the body of a much younger man; there is nothing wrong with him outside of his grouchy and grumpy demeanor.* My sister picked up. I could tell that she was in a hurry, and attempting to keep herself calm and collected.

"What's wrong?" I asked.

"It's Dad. David [our brother] called to check on him during the storm, and when he did not answer the phone, Dave drove over to make sure he was okay. He found Dad lying in bed, unable to get up. He stated that his back hurt, but when Dave went to move him, he passed out. EMT's took him to the hospital, and they say that he has an aortal aneurysm. R.T., it does not look good," she said.

I was at a loss for words. "What are you doing now?" I stuttered.

"I am trying to get a few things together and get up there, right now," she replied.

"Deb, it is night. There is a raging hurricane over your head, and you are four hours away."

"I know. I'll drive safely, and I will call you with any news when I get there. I'm gone." And with that, she hung up.

I stood staring at the phone, in disbelief, for several long minutes; Terry came up to me and asked what was wrong. I tried to explain, but found myself to be at a loss for words. She led me to the couch, whipped up a tall glass of iced tea infused with a touch of an adult beverage, and kept that glass filled for the remainder of the evening. It did little to numb the pain.

I don't recall coming to bed. I can't remember what Terry and I talked about that evening, but my next enduring recollection were my eyes snapping open and staring at the illuminated, bedside clock that read 2:18 a.m. I don't know why I woke up; I don't recall any sounds or stirrings from my bride that would bring me back to the real world. I just woke up and it felt important that I do so. I stared at the clock and thought, *Deb must be there now; I have not heard from her, so no news is surely good news in this case.* And, as thoughts of my father and recently departed mother floated through my soggy mind, the phone rang.

I jumped up, grabbed the cordless phone, and ran out of the room to keep from disturbing Terry. As I turned on the phone and put it to my ear, I felt that I was reliving a scene from several months ago, when I answered a phone only to hear that my mother had lost her battle for life. There was ice in my veins as I uttered a quiet, "Hello?" There was a pause on the other end. It was probably only a second or two, but at that point in time, it lasted for days, and in that silence, I began to fall. I was whirling, spinning, and falling down a dark hole. Standing in that hallway, frozen to the floor, I was dizzy. The inner spinning gave me vertigo; I thought that I might be sick. And then from far away, in a clear and well-controlled voice, I heard my sister say over the phone, "He's gone; they couldn't save him; he felt no pain; Dad is dead." And as the eldest and surely wisest of four children, I rendered an articulate and encouraging response to a woman who has seen, in person, both of her parents die this year. I began to spin deeper into that dark shaft and managed to croak out one word, "Okay," and then hung up.

My spinning turned into tumbling, and the velocity at which I was falling threatened to tear me apart when, all of a sudden, I felt a pair of warm and loving arms embrace me and pull me from the shaft. I opened my eyes to see Terry firmly holding me and hugging me where I stood. Her head was buried in my chest, and I heard a faint and muffled, "I'm so sorry."

She walked me back to the bed and then crawled in while I just sat on my side. When I received the news of my mother's passing, I was sitting on that same bed, staring out the exact same window; and, on the other side had been Harley, staring at me with sad eyes. He knew, he felt my pain, and it was too much for him to bear. I wondered if Harley the wonder horse was there now, looking, feeling, reassuring, so I stood and looked out into the night—nothing. I looked through the darkness of the west pasture for the shaded silhouette for any of the horse children and still, there was nothing. With that, I showered, shaved, and prepared to go to my office, as there was no way to sleep, now. It was only 3:00 a.m. but perhaps I could lose myself in the issues of my profession and keep my mind busy while my heart and soul wrestled with this tragedy.

It was all a daze. Things were blurry, but somehow I managed to get prepared and head out to the garage to fire up Big Red for the trip to my office. The dogs greeted me with their normal cheery "good morning" as I hit the button to raise the garage door. I looked to the east pasture for the horses— nothing. I opened up the truck's door, threw my briefcase on the passenger seat, and then walked over to the barn to see if the horses were sleeping in their covered beach sand rest area— nothing. I could not see them in the back pasture either. *What a difference from the intense contact and feelings on Mom's passing,* I thought. *What a difference.*

I slowly drove down our driveway and pulled out onto the road in front of our farm. I hung a left and headed west. It was misty, foggy, with the moisture clinging to the last four feet closest to the earth. Unbeknownst to me, I was being watched. There was a pair of human eyes in our bedroom window watching the lights of the red dually slowly pull away, and there were several pairs of equine eyes doing the same.

I looked to my left to check the west pasture and saw a dark shadow standing up against the front fence. I slowed to a stop and looked. The glow from one of the barnyard lights revealed the silhouettes of several rounded backs clustered underneath the oak tree in the front of the pasture; they were motionless. And, right before me, at the fence, was the silhouette of the neck and head of a tall, dark horse, Bart. I could not see any features as the light was behind him, but I could see that his head was held high as if he were afraid. Bart resembles a giraffe when he is frightened. I attempted to let my eyes adjust to the darkness and dropped the truck's window. I called out to Harley, first. From under the tree, a round back stirred and a head bobbed up out of the mist. I called to him, "Do you know?" He did not move; he made no sound; he simply lowered his head back into the mist.

My eyes were now better-acclimated to the darkness, and from the side splash of my headlights, I could see Bart's eyes. It was easy now, as the whites of his eyes stood out like a nightlight in the darkness. "Bart, are you okay?" I called into the night. The head went higher. "Do you know? Do you feel the loss?" I asked. His head turned so that just the right eye stared directly at me. "Another part of me has departed," I whispered. And, with that, Bart stomped one time, snorted, hung his head below the mist line, and walked slowly off into misty darkness.

I rolled my window up, pushed on the accelerator, and allowed the cool, dark mist to swallow me up. The darkness brought no comfort.

A CONVERSATION
WITH A HORSE

"Man, it's late!" I muttered as I glanced at my watch while washing my hands in the tack room. On weekends, I don't even wear a watch, as it has no bearing on reality. Things that need to be done get, worked on' and the only reference to time is either the growling of an empty stomach or the disappearance of natural light. Tonight was different. It was a weeknight, and I was trying to get a few small chores accomplished in the barn before calling it a day. For a July night, it was exceptionally hot, and the whirl of the barn's ceiling fans did little to dissipate the heat; in fact, they simply seemed to be re-circulating the hot air.

I quickly dried my hands, turned off the fans, and killed the lights. I stepped out of the barn into the muggy dusk and began to slide the barn's doors closed—there was a rumor that nighttime storms might threaten. As I slid one door closed and then the other, I could feel at least one pair of eyes on me, watching and wondering what it was this human was doing. That feeling of being watched is not an unfamiliar one, as our farm's compound is surrounded on three sides by pastures. Even in the front, equine eyes can see what we are doing at all times. I turned and looked to the east pasture where one lone horse was standing over the water trough, under the light, with a drooping head and his right rear foot cocked. Ethan, the "Sappy Appy," was relaxing over the cool water with one eye peeking between the fence's wooden rails. That one eye that had the perpetual stare of astonishment in it—always watching, always observing.

I hollered, "Hey Ethan," as I walked across the courtyard to the house. One ear picked up.

"What's happening; where are all of your friends?" I asked. He picked his head up and looked directly at me from across the top of the fence. I slowed down my pace.

"Everything all right?" I asked. And, with that, two horse ears zeroed right in on me, and his look intensified. I stopped and turned to walk to him. Of course, the ears pinned back immediately, so I walked a ways down the fence, leaned over, and looked the other way so that he would not feel pressed or put upon. It didn't take but a minute before I could feel the warm, soft breath of a horse on the back of my neck. Slowly, I turned toward him and held out my drink for him to smell. He dropped his head and stared at the darkening ground.

"What's happening?" I asked again. There was a feeling of wanting, a degree of tension in the air, and I could not put my finger on its origin. "Hmmmmmmm?"

With no reply, I then tried a technique that I had been working on for the prior several months. I attempted to send my questions to him without using my mouth. I concentrated and asked how he was doing, again, and projected the emotion in the question. The need for an answer, a desire to communicate, rolled out of me without a sound and splashed on the ground in front of him—still nothing.

Feeling like this was a special moment, as it was rare to have Ethan alone. I closed my eyes and tried the technique again. Then I just listened. I have been trying to talk "to" these guys for ages with marginal results. Maybe it was time for me to shut not only my mouth, but to shut down my mind and just listen for a change. I gave it a shot and tried just to turn "off."

Far away, I could hear a dog bark. There was the rhythmic croaking of the tree frogs, the flutter of insect wings against the overhead courtyard light, and a gentle droning of the universe. Then way off down a deep tunnel, somewhere far, far, away, I heard a quiet voice. I could not understand it, but I could hear it, so I loosened up and let the voice find me.

At first, it was a human-like sound, something akin to distant mumbling. As it sought me out and came closer to me, I could discern its resonance and texture. It was deep and gravely, not melodic or singsong in nature. If it had a gender, it was male and most definitely not female. It was urgent and forceful, yet still I could not understand it. I was reminded of being in a foreign country, listening to an articulate native, not having a clue as to the content of the speech. Then, there was a protracted silence—the type of silence that you hear when you stick cotton in your ears and the only sound is your heart beating far away. It felt as if time stood still. Even my pulse faded away. Until from deep down in the depths of my soul I heard and felt a thundering crash, a smashing sound like glass breaking with the shards falling on a hard tiled floor. The impact of the initial shocking explosion filtered on down to a gentle tinkling like snowflakes settling on an open field in the quiet of a still winter's night.

I was stunned, tingling, vibrating, when I heard, "Can you hear me?"

I jerked my head up, my eyes stared into the darkness, and I quickly spun around. I turned with so much animation that I almost lost my balance. I was shocked to see the spooky Appaloosa still standing calmly, gazing at the ground. Normally, such a move would have sent him bolting across the pasture. I looked towards the house—no one. I looked all around, and it was just Ethan and me.

"Gee you're jumpy, and you call me spooky!" I jumped backwards, tripped, and promptly landed on my butt, staring back at the horse. The voice came from *inside* my head. It was clear, concise, and totally understandable.

"Am I losing my mind?" I thought.

"You lost that fight a long time ago, but that's another story," was the reply.

I sat there in the grass, numb to everything but that one eye of the Appaloosa staring at me from behind the fence with a knowing look.

"Is that you, Ethan?" I asked.

"I don't know. Names don't mean much to horses, but if you are asking the horse that is standing in front you, that would be me," came the reply.

"How come I understand you, how do you know English?" I inquired.

"You are not hearing me in English as you are not hearing, you are feeling from within. And, because I am communicating with you, through you, you hear me in a way that you understand. Therefore, it is understood as English, representing all the words that you have in your memory and vocabulary. It is how your mind works—not mine, but yours. You can stand up, now, as the grass is wet. I know since you make me sleep on it every night instead of letting me into that nice, dry stall in the barn," the horse complained.

"That's so that you can continue to eat and not be trapped in a cell all night. You know how you like to graze, eat, eat, eat that is your middle—Hey, what am I doing, arguing with a horse?" I countered while scratching my head.

"You are arguing with yourself, and I don't have time to play your human games. I am here for a reason, and I don't know if I will ever have this opportunity again. I have been trying to get through to you for years, but you are so one-sided and never shut up. You continually shower us with words and feelings, but you never listen. How do you expect us to respect you or care about what you say when you give us no respect? You never listen to our answers to your questions. You never, ever, tried to listen; you always talked, talked, talked. You have no idea how annoying you can be."

"But tonight you linked, finally, because you stopped talking for a microsecond and let me in, allowed me inside. I am going to talk fast as there is a lot to share and you have to attempt to absorb what is said. You have a job, a mission, a very special one, and I have been sent here to share that with you."

"I know that you realize that modern man's soul is in trouble; I know as I can feel it in your heart. But, you are not aware of the depth and breadth of the problem."

"Modern man has embraced all of his technology and, in so doing, has isolated himself from the natural world, the real living and breathing world that surrounds us and is all that we are. This has not always been the case with mankind. Early man, even up to this land's native humans, were aware that everything is tied together in a giant, interconnected loop of life. Man, animal, plant, earth, everything is interdependent upon the other. The tribal pulls that you feel tell you that early man was very much in tune with the spirituality of all living creatures. Native humans looked at the animals around them and respected them for the sentient beings that they were. They communed with these beings; they worshiped these spirits and revered their existence while accommodating their wishes. If it became necessary for the existence of the native humans to take the body of another being for food, they held ceremonies and communicated with the spirit of that body to request permission. The beings always obliged and considered it an honor to donate their earthly shell to the humans so that they could move on to a new body and a new experience. Life is about learning; we are here for a reason. You are a man for a reason, and I am a horse for yet a different reason."

"And why am I here as a human?" I asked.

"You don't listen very well; I asked you to pay attention to what I am telling you and to limit your questions. But being that you have broken my train of thought, I will answer your question," the horse responded.

"Man, you sound a lot like me," I quipped.

"I *am* you. If you will just shut up long enough, I will tell you that you are here for a mission, one singular mission that will make a significant mark on the world as a whole. The spirituality of the world is quivering with a shift that you are required to make. There are many like you scattered around the world with this mission, and all of you have been in training for years. The time has come to step out of the classroom and exercise the skills that we have been teaching you," sighed the horse.

"Teaching me? Who has been teaching me? You said "we" have been teaching you; who is we?" I asked.

"I am sure that you already know. You just have not admitted to yourself that every being around you is present for a reason, for one singular lesson that you needed to learn. When you come home, the class begins. We are the professors, and you are the student," he stated.

"Are you saying that you horses are involved in this process?" I asked.

"We *are* the process. Does that surprise you? You haven't figured that out by now? You are the one who stands in that dark window every morning and talks to us. Do you think all of this is just some random mistake? Not so. There is a plan, and all of us are working, together, to bring that plan to fruition," he said.

"Then tell me. What are you here to teach me?" I prodded.

"Me? That I will save for last as you need to be softened up a bit before you get to me, but I will go down the list of my friends and herd mates and explain to you what each and every one of them is here to do. Each one of them has one job, one lesson. Now, see if you have learned them all.

"First, my good buddy, the big gray guy—you know, the one who used to race."

"Harley," I interrupted.

"Remember, we don't do names; we know each other by this form of communication: smell and touch. So, back to my buddy, he is here to teach you how to play. It is his job to show you that even beings inside bodies with four legs need to play. He is of the opinion that you have forgotten how to do that. So, that is why he steals things from you, runs around, and pesters the daylights out of us. You need to learn how to play and have fun," he said.

I could only smile to that account, as it was so true. Harley loves to sneak up behind me, catch my cell by the antenna, and twirl it around his head. If I am working on the fence in the pasture, he will sneak up, grab my toolbox, and run all over the pasture scattering my tools to the four corners of his world. "He is the first to run, jump, and to come to the fence when you walk out the door." I could see all that.

"On to the big brown guy, the one that you work with and fall off of so often," he said.

"Bart," I interjected.

"Whatever. He really loves you, you know. And it pains him to teach you the lesson that he is trying to get through to you because he knows that it has hurt you. But it seems to have jogged your feelings, and he is relieved that he is getting through at last," the horse sighed.

"Getting through, what do you mean? He is the one responding to the new training techniques, not me," I argued.

"That's because you are beginning to use the skills he taught you and that is the way he is letting you know. His assignment was to teach you that you could communicate, as we are doing now. You are always sending signals and images that all sentient beings can pick up. If those signals are controlled and the being is aware that he is transmitting, it can be a very good thing, just as we are communing now. If the transmitting being is unaware of the ability, then it can be a mess of jumbled up, negative, destructive images being sent out into a world that has no room for such feelings. You, for one, were always very bad about that, but you are now improving," the horse said.

"What do you mean?" I asked.

"You carry quite a few scars around on your body due to your encounters with the big brown one. Remember when he came back from training school several years ago, back when you and the big brown one would partner up and you would climb on his back and ride around?" asked the horse.

"Yes, I remember. I miss those times, as since then he has done nothing but buck me off and try to kill me," I countered.

"No, he did not want to hurt you and he never stepped on you, so get that out of your head. Remember back when you used to get him ready to climb on his back? What sort of thoughts ran through your mind?" he inquired.

"Hmmmmm, I knew that he had been trained well. I was excited to have him home and looked forward to going riding with him, to being able to share experiences. I remember nothing but good things and positive thoughts," I said.

"And how did the session go?"

"Great! No problems. We had lots of fun!" I added.

"Exactly," countered the horse. "That's what I am talking about! Now, do you recall that you did not ride him for almost a year; and, when you were preparing to crawl on his back, after all that time, what sort of thoughts were running through your head?" he asked.

"I was deeply concerned that he may be unmanageable, spooky, and potentially dangerous. I sincerely was scared of him," I remembered.

"And what happened?" he asked.

"After a few seconds he exploded straight up in the air, which resulted in me landing flat on my back and the crunching of several ribs. I still have not recovered 100%," I mumbled.

"Right. You waited yet another year to try again, and what were your thoughts then?"

"That time I was certain that he would explode, so I prepared myself by getting in the saddle, holding on, and waiting for the explosion. I was going to stay on that time."

"And what happened?"

"He exploded, and I stayed on. But then, he fell down on his front legs and we both fell forward to the ground."

"You don't know how hard it was for him to avoid landing right on top of you. He barely managed to avoid hurting you further. My point here is this, short and sweet—you got what you expected. When you were projecting pictures and feelings of confidence, you got exactly what you wanted. When you were sending images to the big brown one of falling, or running and bucking, he gave you exactly what he thought you wanted. You asked for it, and he gave it to you. It doesn't get any simpler than that."

"Remember last week, when you were out in the barn late? You let all of the rest of us out except for the big brown one. What happened that night that was different?"

"Well," I thought. "I had not been able to get a saddle on him for ages so I just took my time, tacked him up, told him how good he was just standing there in the center aisle of the barn, and then took everything off."

"Did he buck, did he show any nervousness? No. I was watching and, by now, you should know why."

"Again, I had no intention of getting up on him so I was not nervous. There was no need to be, as I had in my mind that I was just going to tack him up and then dress him down. So, are you saying that because I did not project a feeling or image of fear he was fine? Do you mean that he gave me just what I wanted as I was sending a picture of him just standing there calmly while I played with him?" I asked.

"Doink! What took you so long, genius?" he laughed.

"Horses don't use words like 'doink,'" I fussed.

"Hey, it's in your head; it is what your mind chose to use for a translation, not me. I don't have a clue except that I am abashed at how long it took you to figure that out. The big brown one has been giving you everything that you have been telling him you wanted for years. It created great problems for him and much stress, since he loves to be with you and you keep telling him to throw you off of him. Haven't you noticed that he has to eat twice as much as the rest of us to keep his weight on? Do you know what causes that? It is stress, my human friend, stress that you cause by sending the wrong signals to those around you."

"Now, has the big brown one made his point and can we consider this lesson to have been learned, since it is a very important one to get right before we move on?" He lifted his head and looked straight at me for a reaction.

"Yes, yes. I feel rather stupid for not picking up on it sooner. But, put into the terms that you just shared with me, I feel blessed to know this. The idea of being able to communicate is exciting, it's blinking awesome." I chuckled like a child who had just found his Christmas present under the tree.

"That ability has always been there, as it is in all humans. But, with modern man, it is shut away and not allowed to be recognized. Your young humans are aware of this, as you once were, but it is quickly pushed down and turned off by the adult humans around them. However, it is always there, just below the surface for all humans, and it works on humans, too. Have you ever had your female say something to you that you were thinking about at just that moment? And with all of your divine intellectual capacity, you just chalk it off to coincidence. Talk about being a lower life form—good grief. I know salamanders that are quicker than that," he chuckled.

"All right, all right. Point taken," I waved my hands in frustration. "What is Apache's lesson?"

"Who is Apache?" he asked.

"Sigh." This was getting tiresome. "The little gray guy from another land; we brought him back from Brazil."

"Yes, the little gray one. His nationality means nothing to us, as he is one in the heart. He has traveled all this way to teach you of devotion. Years ago in a land far away, your female whispered into his ear that she would not leave him to an uncertain future. She kept her promise, and now, he keeps his. He does not have to be touched, ridden, or noticed for months, but when your female wants him to work for her, he is there—without question. The devotion he feels is deeper than the human heart can comprehend. He will never falter," said the horse.

"Well, that takes care of all the other horses. How about you?" I asked.

"You confuse me; how about the little brown mare? She is here for a reason, do you not know what it is?" he asked.

"She is here only temporarily: a foster horse. We need to find her a forever home so that she will never have to be moved again. She does not count, like you guys, as she is only temporary," I answered.

"She most certainly does count, and that is exactly why she is here! She knows she is temporary, but because of the good things you have done for her, she has grown to love you both. It is her job to teach you that it is okay to break down that wall and love someone even though it is only for a short time. You must risk the pain when it comes time to leave to enjoy the moment of love that you can share right now. She risks that hurt for you, and in so doing, she is attempting to show you that it is okay to love her back. She so wants you and your female to let go and enjoy the relationship that you could all have."

I paused for a moment as that one smarted. I had been holding the little bay Arab at arm's length, as I was afraid to enjoy her company and get close to her. It would hurt so much when it came time to let her go. It had been difficult to do so. Now that I knew she was going the extra mile, it was time for me to let go and open up.

"Okay, I am beginning to get the point. But, how about you? What has been your lesson?" I asked.

"Ha! It is almost stupid for me to continue, as you already know why I am here. You have seen it, and you have already used me as an example. I am here to show you that we can all change; we can all learn and improve ourselves. Was I not the first horse you rescued in this land?" he asked.

"Yes," I replied.

"Was I not fearful, spooky, grouchy, and mean?"

"Yes."

"Am I that way now?"

"No, quite the contrary."

"I changed. I showed you that I could change, and in demonstrating that, you have too. What you do not know is why I was afraid, why I was mean, why I was spooky. I was all of those things because my life, as a horse, was a miserable existence. A young human female loved me, once, and I thought my life would be complete forever. Sadly, as she approached adulthood, her thoughts and love turned towards human males and she forgot me. She left me standing in my stall for weeks without visiting. The only attention I received was from the stable hands, who fed me and cleaned my small stall. It hurt, it ached, and I grew fearful. You have never known fear until you have felt it in the body of a horse. Every cell screams, and there is no control over it; it is a physical presence that takes on a personality of its own. And, in that fear, I grew defensive and mean."

"I was then passed around to several male humans, who wanted me to work, but I fought them and they fought back with spurs, bits, whips, and even sticks. I learned to hate all manmade implements and found that if I resisted, the human would eventually give up and go away. That is what happened before you came into my world. They left me at a stable and just moved away—no food, no nothing. So, the human who lived there turned me out into a pasture. The next thing I knew, I was at an auction, and there you were. I didn't much like you at first, but I had a mission, and you made it easy for me. You and your female have treated me with kindness and gentleness, and you have made it easy for me to demonstrate change. Here we are today, both you and me, completing our assignments and moving on," said the horse.

"Wait, wait, wait," I interrupted. "Are you telling me it was some sort of divine plan that you ended up with us and we are where we are right now? That is a little far-fetched don't you think?"

"Had you ever gone to a horse auction before?" he asked.

"No."

"Have you ever been to one since then?"

"No."

"Did you and your female not feel a pull towards me?"

"Yes."

"Did I not appear to be everything you always wanted in a horse and showered you with affection at the auction?"

"Yes, but you promptly turned into a real work of art when we got you home."

"Hey, mission accomplished! I got done what needed to be done, and then the lessons began," he said.

My head was spinning with all of this information. I was actually dizzy and leaned against the fence for stability. Ethan, the horse, gently set his chin down on my right elbow and sighed. I heard him say, "Are you ready for the mission that we have been preparing you for?"

"What could that possibly be, my friend? What sort of mission am I destined to fulfill?" I asked.

The horse paused, as if to reflect and attempt to put his thoughts in the proper order.

"You are already on the road to your destiny by taking little steps towards it each day. You have been building a network of contacts, gathering the information, practicing on a small scale, but not taking that major jump. You are almost there, but you need to take the leap, step through the threshold, and make it so."

I was getting a little frustrated at this point, as it seemed as if he were beating around the bush. "So, tell me. Don't flower it up or make it fancy, just give me the facts!"

"The facts are," he continued, "that the scales of the universe have been tipped in a very negative way. Humans have tipped them. The world has not seen such a horrendous shift since the slaughter of the buffalos or the butchering of our brother whales in the sea. Humans have taken, once again, to butchering innocent beings for nothing more than greed. They are slaying special, trusting, self-aware lives only for something that you call money. A true holocaust is happening right here in the land that we live. Healthy, young, sentient beings are being slaughtered for food for people in foreign lands. These beings helped settle your country and were your means of transportation since the dawn of time, your companions and friends. To have that trust violated in such a manner has sent shock waves across our universe. The crime is horse slaughter, my friend. Beings like my herd brethren and me are being killed only for meat in a most cruel and painful way. Their poor spirits are so shattered and splintered when they cross over that they cannot be repaired. They cannot be healed. They are destined to scream with agony, fear, and rage for all eternity, as there is nothing that can match this violation of love and trust. It pains me to relay this information to you, as there is no way for you to comprehend this sort of spiritual fear. It far supersedes the physical fear that I spoke of earlier. This fear and anger become a world within themselves, and it can poison all that come into contact with it. The carnage must stop! It has to stop. That is what *you* have to do. *You* have to stop it!" He fell silent.

I had rested my head on my hands atop the fence as he spoke. It had gotten very dark and still. I could feel screams of pain and fear ringing in my ears. Suddenly, I was aware of being bumped, jostled, and stepped on. There was confusion everywhere. We were being forced down a chute, single file, with blood-curdling screams echoing all around. The smell of fear and death clouded my mind. Screams—many were mine. The numbers in front of me diminished until I stood alone in front of a dark, solid metal door. There were noises and thuds, kicking and clunking. The door callously slid open as a searing pain burned me from behind. I jumped into a tight space that was slick with urine and feces—the smell, the fear. A hand with something in it swung at my head. I ducked, and there was a horrible thud and pain in my neck. I tried to rear up to escape and fell. The thing dove for my head again as I struggled to get up. Who was doing this? What had I done?

What was happening? I ducked again and a thundering crash shattered the side of my face. I could feel the bones break; the stunning numbness rang out from the wound like a gong hit with a hammer. I fought back and tried to regain my footing; I screamed for help, but there was no answer. I was alone, alone fighting to live—"Betrayed," flashed through my mind when the bolt finally found my forehead. And, as if my body was a fine, porcelain figurine, I crumbled and crashed to the filthy floor.

Move, move, move, and run ran through my mind; but there was no moving when a cable was attached to my right rear leg and I felt myself being hoisted up by my back foot. The weight of all of my internal organs on my lungs forced the breath out of my stunned and battered body. I could feel ligaments snap in my leg and the crackling of the stressed cartilage in my knee was audible. Why? Why? Why? There were only shapes in my field of vision, and the blade of the knife felt cold as it slashed across my throat. My blood was warm as it poured down my head and mouth. As the blood flowed, an unnatural cold began to creep into my body, and it brought no peace. *Why, what had I done, where was the love, where were my people?* I was slipping down into a dark vortex of sadness and despair until my soul shattered into a million pieces as the last drop of blood left my now still heart.

I felt the scream curdle up my throat like hot molten magma about to erupt, when a familiar voice in my head said, "It is not your time; it is not you; your job is clear, and you must make it so."

I picked up my head and attempted to inhale. My throat was raw as if I had been screaming for hours and my eyes were clouded with tears, when I looked up at Ethan. I was shaking, my clothes were soaked, and a fleeting human thought hoped that it was from sweat only. I gagged and threw up before I could get out the word. "How?"

"Tell them, tell them all what it is like. You know the humans to tell. Many are waiting for you to speak up and join them, just tell them and make it so."

"How do I tell them? What do I do?" I sobbed.

"Tell them this story, tell them what I have told you, and tell them all. They are waiting for you; now, tell them!"

"I can't tell them that, I can't!" as I choked on my own words.

"You have no choice, it is your destiny. We have seen ours through without excuses, now the reins have been passed to you. Tell them and they will understand. It is the *Force of the Horse*. Tell them, my friend, as time is short. Tell them, as hundreds are killed every day. Those who die are calling to you and you can hear them. Tell the humans, as there has never been a grander stand to make than the one you need to make now. Tell them the story and they shall know."

He hung his head and whispered, "You use the phrase 'May the horse be with you,' and you do so as your heart knows the truth; the horse is with you now. Tell them with your pen, write the right words, and tell them the bloodshed must stop. We shall be with you—tell them." And, with that, he softly turned and started to disappear into the darkness.

"Wait!" I cried. "I need more help. I cannot believe our own cruelty. I have more questions, please!"

Through my tears, in the darkness, I could just make out that the horse had turned his head my way. From far, far away I heard the distant voice whisper, "There is no time, tell them!"

With a soft sigh, the horse slipped off into the darkness, leaving me alone on the grass, sobbing as I have never sobbed before.

"Tell them," I whispered between gasps. "It is my destiny."

THE FORCE OF
THE HORSE – PART III

I turned over the water trough in the back pasture so that I could clean it, and the water washed over my sandaled feet. Ah, the water on my bare feet felt good. Not the safest way to work around horses, but I wasn't going to get too up close and personal this afternoon.

Once the water was on the ground, I began to scrub the insides to remove all of the algae. I then noticed that a few of our equine children came over to investigate. Of course, Harley was first to walk over and paw at the puddle. This was a new game. When it rains, he hunts out the first puddle and paws at it as if digging. My wife was certain that he was digging for crawfish. Bart followed, but kept his distance. You know, water puddles have been known to attack horses in the past, or at least that is what was on his mind. Ethan attempted to drink. I looked over while righting the trough and said, "This will be full in a few minutes, guys. Clean, fresh, cool water." The automatic valve was already allowing a steady and noisy stream of water into the trough, so noisy that Bart stepped back a few paces.

I reached for the fence to jump back over when I was interrupted with, "Well, how did it go?" Dang, I let go of the fence and spun around so fast that Bart bolted off into the distance and Harley almost lost his footing in the mud trying to get away. And, standing like a statue without a flinch was Ethan.

"I hate it when you do that. You don't know how terrifying it is to have a voice just pop up into your head out of nowhere. Can't you warn me when you are about to do that?" I growled at him.

"Hey, we do what we can do, when we can do it. You have been filling my head with stupid images and unorganized thoughts for years. With all of the garbage that flows out of you, I had serious doubts that you were even salvageable. It appears that the jury may still be out on the verdict," he said.

"I don't come out to work with and see you guys to get insulted. I can stay on the other side of the fence, if that's what I was after."

"Feisty today, aren't we?" he said. "I thought that you had a rule about being 'together' before you entered our domain. Did that fly out the window?"

"No, no," I stammered. "Man you are good, now you have me apologizing to you. No, it's just that I have not slept much since you last spoke to me. With what you revealed, I cannot rest. My wife or 'my female' rarely even sleeps with me now due to the fitful situation I struggle with all night. You were right, I hear them; and putting my hands over my ears while humming does not make it go away. What will make it stop?" I pleaded.

"That's why I asked how it was going. Have you told them?" he asked.

"Yes, I told them your story."

"And how many did you tell?"

"A couple hundred; all I could think of telling."

"And how many humans live in this land?"

"Several hundred million," I sighed.

"Sounds to me as if you have barely started," he exclaimed.

"Easy for you to say; you don't have the burden of dealing with multiple human personalities that are all intertwined with egos, agendas, wants, needs, etc."

"True. That is why I was not selected to perform your part of the mission. That is up to you and as you have found out; there is no going back."

"Going back is not the issue," I said. "What do I need to do to go forward?"

"Tell you what, you look a little frazzled. Go and get one of your human flavored drinks. I will take a nice long draw from the fresh water you just supplied, and I will meet you under the pecan tree. I think you could use a little horse sense. Sound like a plan?" he asked.

"Works for me," I said, as I climbed over the fence and headed for the outside kitchen where the ingredients for my world famous Wrangler Iced Tea were located.

I was back out in the pasture in only a few moments. All of the other horses had shifted off to the west, but Ethan was standing under one of the pecan trees with his head into the breeze and his left rear foot cocked. As I walked up to him, I rubbed his withers.

"I would appreciate a little stomach scratch, if you don't mind," he said. "It would put me into more of a thoughtful mood. Ahhhhhhhhhhhh," he groaned, as I scratched right in the center of his stomach, one of those spots that no horse can reach.

"I always figured that you liked that spot scratched as you make goofy faces; but this is the first time I have ever *heard* you enjoy it," I smiled.

"Mmmunph" was all that came back as he stretched out his neck and made that silly face that always cracks me up.

"There are times when you don't look too cool, also, particularly, when the big brown one drags you around the pasture by a rope. You also are pretty funny when you fall off. I have noticed that it takes you longer and longer to get up with each fall. Could you be getting older or are you getting smarter?" he laughed.

"Boy, for a horse you have one heck of a caustic sense of humor," I said.

"Remember, your mind puts it together in a way that you understand. Perhaps you have the warped sense of humor and not me. As a rule, we laugh very little, but you humans give us a lot of reasons to giggle. It's what you call a 'whinny'." he chuckled.

"All right," I said, between sips of tea. "I really appreciate you wanting to talk to me. You left me in the grass, alone, at night, terrified from what I had learned. I have felt so alone and helpless ever since. Having you here, now, makes me feel better, makes it feel more real." I talked as I stroked his neck and back. He appeared to be enjoying the attention.

"I am glad that you feel better through this talk; but I will warn you, we have a job to do. It is to teach you about us: us horses and how we live, love, and communicate. That is what we have taught you, and we have given you a mission that must be accomplished. Being that we are horses and you are human, our advice and input on how to accomplish that mission in a world of humans is going to be very limited, at best."

"I can appreciate that. My problem or dilemma is just that—how do we get the message across to the humans; how do we get them to listen; and once they have heard, what can we do to motivate them to act and to move forward? I guess my biggest problem is that I don't have the answer on how to make humans care. That comes from within, not from being forced. I cannot make another human care if they do not have the inclination to do so."

"Ahhh," said Ethan, "then it appears that you have answered your own question. If humans need to develop a caring response and it has to come from within, then you cannot talk to their minds. You will have to speak to their hearts and cultivate that feeling from within them."

"Easier said than done," I answered.

"Don't discount your abilities," he countered. "You have some very powerful and insightful friends who are trying to do the same thing. They have the same mission, and you need to join forces with them, as your power of influence will be increased exponentially. Give it a shot."

"Exponentially? Where did that come from? I never use the word 'exponentially'."

"You fail to give yourself proper credit," he chuckled.

"For being such an old grouch, you can be pretty cool at times."

"We all have our moments," he snorted. "Speak with your friends, form a plan, and then work the plan. I am confident that you all working together will make it happen. You have to make it happen, as there are no options. You watch silly media things about the conclusion of the world from forces outside of this universe. I have a news flash for you: The conclusion of this world will not be brought about by powers from the outside. The end will come from the malignant and evil powers from within. You need to stop this one evil. It may not seem like much to some, and it may seem like too much to others, but by stopping this killing, you will have started to turn the tide back to the positive side and the scales will become balanced. If this does not occur, the downhill slide of humanity will accelerate. It is really up to you all. Those who are standing in the pens, waiting to be slaughtered, know that there are a handful of humans out there fighting for them. It does not reduce their terror, and it does not comfort them; but there is a pinpoint of hope for those that follow, and even that much makes a difference."

"You leave me speechless," I said.

"Now go back to work. Do whatever a human does to excite, motivate, and elevate other humans to do what is right and just. Go do your human thing and make it so."

"All right," I said, as I swallowed another swig of tea. "I am on my way; and, please, say 'hello' to the other guys for me."

"That reminds me," said Ethan, "Harley wants you to know that everything is alright. He said that you would know what that meant, so I will not explain. It is hot. I need another drink," he muttered. With that, he walked off towards the water trough while I slid my back down the pecan tree until I was sitting on the ground beneath it. *Harley said that everything is alright* rang in my ears. I looked out across the pasture at the grazing horses. Harley had his head turned toward me. Tears began to blur my vision, and I could barely make out when he went back to grazing.

SHE STOLE MY HEART

She came to us while in a foreign land, far, far away. Yet, she was not native to the country where she was born. Her father was from Belgium and her mother was from the United States, but she was born in Brazil. A multinational before she even opened her eyes.

The first time I laid eyes upon little Niki, I was in love in five seconds flat. A little ball of fur with grown up German Shepherd markings. For a male to say "too cute for words" is a bit of a stretch; nonetheless, I said the phrase many times, as we played with this little jolly globe of fluff.

Her "godfather" was a swashbuckling friend of ours from Belgium. Captain Koen had a Flemish accent that was so strong, his English was almost unintelligible to the untrained ear. However, Captain Koen had a heart for animals, as do we. Niki was the pick of the litter, and we took her home before potential parents viewed any of the puppies. Niki was our new "daughter," a blessing and ray of sunshine in a third-world country. She brought us great joy.

Niki was intended to be Terry's companion as she was held in Expatriate prison during the years that we lived in Brazil. Thousands of miles from home, she was stuck in a meager little house. Terry could not clean and was not allowed to cook. We had a full time maid. And, when it came to gardening, her attempts to make a change in the tropical foliage were thwarted by the gardener. I, on the other hand, had an office to go to every day, but for Terry, it was different.

Once she had completed her second degree, there was little for an intelligent American woman to do in Brazil. Terry had brought her cat, Blizzard, down from the U.S. Cats, however, are not much for conversing, nor are they interested in going for walks on the beach. Niki was to be all of that and more.

Niki lived with us for only a month when Terry went back to the U.S. for an extended visit. In reality, she was running away from the great 2000 Millennium scare and left Niki and me alone in Brazil to fend for ourselves. I know that she lost on that bet as New Year's Eve 2000 on the beach of Macaé, Brazil, was the biggest party I have ever attended. In all reality, it took a day or two in bed to recognize that fact. But, while Terry was gone, I cheated: I let Niki in the house; I let Niki lie with me on the couch and watch TV; I took Niki for rides in the car, even though she got motion sickness from the cobblestone streets and puked at every turn. Niki bonded with me. We were "father" and "daughter."

When the time came to come back to the U.S., Terry brought back her horse, Apache, and I brought back my dog, Niki. Needless to say, the cat came along for the flight, as well.

We were an interesting lot coming through immigration in Miami.

Niki has always been there. She grew up to be one of the most gorgeous "plush" German Shepherds that anyone had ever seen. Her heart was as big as Texas and her love for me pushed to the point of being manic and sometimes, unsettling. Whenever I was on our property, she had to be able to see me, even when I went inside the house, those dark sentient eyes always watching and, in her mind, protecting me. She was deathly afraid that the horses would hurt me, so she paced and barked anytime I was in the barn or the round pen. It was not always appreciated, but, other times, it felt good to have that pair of eyes trained on me at all times. At least someone cared; somebody was watching.

There are a hundred stories to tell, both good and a few bad, but there is no longer any point in telling them. It is now all over, as Niki is dead. She was just five years old when something in her healthy body gave out. She just lay down to sleep one night and never got back up. Another bit of my soul had left and even more emptiness had crept in. Little Niki was forever gone.

In a matter of a several months, Terry and I lost my mother, my mother's sister, my father, Terry's grandmother, and now my dog Niki. I know that it is not deemed appropriate to discuss the death of a dog alongside the passing of a human family member; but, for Terry and me, who do not have two-legged children, our cat, dogs (now dog), and horses are our children. Now, one of the youngest and most vital had left us. My heart was broken, as she was the first to greet me every morning and the first to welcome me home at the end of the day. We have her mate, Kenny, and it kills us to see him search for her and call out, as he too misses her.

This is not profound. There is no great spiritual message either affixed or hidden in these words. I am too numb and tired to be that clever. This is nothing more than an attempt to say "goodbye" in an effort to close yet another chapter; a plea for release, as I never knew that a broken heart could cause physical pain; and, lastly, an outcry for peace.

She was beautiful, she was special, we loved her dearly, and we miss her so. Goodbye, Niki. Rest peacefully as we hope to see you again. And, as I walk this property, I know that your spirit is still here, watching, laughing, and guarding me. You did a great job and worked hard. We love you and miss you. Now, my daughter, please rest. Dad loves you.

HORSE WHISPERS

The wind was blowing out of the north and it was almost 11:00 p.m. on a night in mid-November in Texas. It was bone chilling cold.

It was Friday night, November 12, 2004, the night before our rescue's annual Horse Festival fundraiser at the Brenham County Fairgrounds. We were trying to put the finishing touches on all that needed to be accomplished before the gates opened up at 9:00 a.m. the following morning.

We had completed our member Appreciation Dinner, which consisted of delivered Domino's pizza and Coke. Once finished, the majority of the members had filtered off to warm motel/hotel rooms to prepare for the day to follow. Only a few die-hards remained, and the only reason that I was still there was because Terry was one of those die-hards. Anything hard or strong in me had died an hour or so earlier, and I was dragging...badly.

Terry and I had pulled two of our equine charges with us, all the way from Louisiana, so that they could participate in the event. Apache was to be ridden (that's a story in its own right) in the Parade of Breeds. We brought along our foster horse, Maleeva, the cute little Arabian mare that has lived with us for ten months, so that she could have a new foster home in Texas, where her odds of being adopted and finding her forever home were much greater. So, we had company for the ride and equine children to take care of while in Brenham.

It appeared that the evil, slave-driving wives were about to wind down. So, I informed Terry that I was going down to the horse barn to check on the horses. We had experienced an earlier problem when Apache and Maleeva were not stalled near each other. The quiet, laid-back Apache was very distraught and wanted to be near "his" little Maleeva. Therefore, we had moved them into back-to-back stalls so that they would be together during the weekend. I walked down the hill and into the barn where there were stalls for over 100 horses—only about 30–40 were over-nighting before the big day. During the course of the afternoon, there had been a great deal of commotion and excitement in the barn. As I neared in the quiet of the night, I could tell that everyone had settled in for sleeping time and there were no pressing issues.

I calmly walked into the barn that was housing all those equine souls and knew within three steps that I was about to live one of those "life experiences." I immediately slowed down my pace so that I could savor the event. The smell of the hay, horse poop, feed, and the gentle breathing of the horses blended into a heady concoction of pure relaxation and contentment. I slowly strolled down one aisle, headed towards Maleeva, and passed the calm and relaxed horses that were gently falling asleep. I was the only human amongst them, yet they felt confident enough with my presence not to look, flinch, or open an eye. I smiled as I was accepted and trusted to be one of them. I knew this was going to be special.

I reached little Maleeva's stall only to find that she was lying down, dog style, gently dozing, and looking just as cute and peaceful as she could. Pressed up against the back bars of her stall, on the other side, was Apache, standing, watching her as if he were on guard with his eyes half-lidded. He was struggling to stay awake and never bothered to lift his head to look at me. He was staring at Maleeva. This was all rather odd, as he would not give her the time of day back home. He had been rude and very pushy with her. One of the reasons we had brought her here was so that she could perhaps find a foster home that was not full of spoiled, pushy geldings.

So, I stood for a few moments and soaked in the feeling. I watched Apache breathe. I watched him blink as he looked at Maleeva. And, I could see that there was a cute, little smile on her equine lips. I watched; I stopped thinking; and then I listened as the whispers pierced my soul.

It was not the wind playing games in the rafters; it was not the fatigue that ate at my bones. It was nearby whispers that I heard—words that I could just make out. As I stared at Apache, the mumbling cleared and I could begin to hear him whisper in a most passionate tone:

"I love you," he said. "You are the world to me, and I am sorry. I did not show you how much you meant to me while back home. The future is always uncertain, but I am so sorry. I will never leave you or take you for granted again. I will guard you and protect you from the others. I am sorry. You are my life. I love you so." Then he sighed. She smiled and sighed, too. Even female horses like to hear words of endearment. I smiled, also, as the little mare looked so content, so peaceful, and so happy to hear and feel such things. Inside I began to struggle with my feelings knowing that they would no longer be together. They were about to be separated and there would be no tomorrows for them as a pair.

As I began to slip back into human mode, the horse whispers caught me again and pulled me back to the place of peace. However, it was not Apache who whispered. It was the gelding next to Maleeva. He was whispering his story. He wanted to speak of his past and he wished for a better life in the future. As I stepped in front of his stall, he began to tell me his story. As he spoke, I read the sign on his door that gave a human's perspective of what he was and where he had been. They did not quite match up as the human story left out the details of abuse and neglect. So, I listened and I smiled. I wished him well and moved on to the mare beside him. She was whispering her tale of woe to a mare behind her and together they compared notes. Both of them were glad to be where they were. They were confident that they were loved. I moved on, out of range of their private conversation.

Stall-by-stall, one-by-one, I listened to each and every one and read their stories, all of them, not one could be missed. There was joy, fear, hate, love, anger, confusion, and depression; but, above all else, there was hope. The feeling of hope was so thick in that cold barn that night that you could have cut it with a knife. The feeling was so real that it stuck to everything like molasses and slowed my pace even further. I drank it in and could feel it purge my soul of any uncertainties or conflicts. There was hope. If my arms were big enough to reach around and collectively give all of those whispering horses a hug at one time, I would have done it. Instead, one-by-one, I listened and reassured them. We were all one for a moment in time. We had the same vision. We had the same smile. And, we had the same heart. It is hope that brings us home.

WE WERE THERE

It was like any other evening feeding of the horses, yet it was not, or not quite, as something was different. The air was crisp and cool as Christmas was only a week away in South Louisiana, but the feeling had little to do with temperature or barometric pressure. There was an electric buzz in the air, the feeling of white noise just outside the audible range of the human ear. There was something tangible and moving in the barn that night.

I did not pick up on it at first. Terry was off having an early Christmas with her family in Florida, which meant that the barn chores and the feeding of all our four-legged children rested upon me when I returned home from my office in the evenings. And, at this time of year, it was already dark. It was a matter of rushing home; putting the vehicle up for the night; greeting and playing with Kenny, the white German Shepherd who gets so excited to see you that he bounces three feet high; dashing into the house to turn on lights; checking messages; changing clothes; feeding the cat; then back outside to dribble the bouncing dog; and into the barn to prepare dinner for the equine boys.

Tonight the wind was not blowing out of the north, so I opened up the big sliding barn doors that look up our drive so that Kenny could look in and watch me. He cannot venture inside, as the invisible fence keeps the big dogs out of the barn both for their safety and for ours.

I scurried into the tack room, flipped on all of the lights, and turned up the radio. Christmas music was the order of the day. As I carefully measured varied degrees of hoof supplement and rice bran with their normal pelletized feed, the thought crossed my mind that my parents, especially my mother, never had the opportunity to see our equine kids nor experience this extraordinary special side to our otherwise very busy lives. I paused from humming along with the radio and reflected on what a tremendous loss that was. Then I questioned whether or not it was a loss for her or a loss for me. My ego subsided, my heart took over, and I realized that it was a loss for me that I would have to ponder and bear, but I would not allow it to rule my life. I resumed mixing and humming, with a small pang of sadness in my heart.

I went from stall to stall filling up the appropriate feed bins with the proper amount of food. Each time I exited a stall and went back to the tack room, I asked Kenny how he was doing as he sat attentively out in the driveway. This inquiry would start the bouncing. I'll never figure out how a 100 lb. dog could bounce so high. He made me laugh. I was just about finished with the mix of the last meal when the traditional and expected three measured knocks came to the back door. Terry and I have learned to keep the back "horse" door closed until ready to let the horses in, as it is such a pleasure to hear those three distinct and perfectly timed and executed knocks.

We knew who it was. He does such a good job at it. It was Ethan. He was the King of Knocking, the Guardian of the Food Gate, and the funniest of them all at feeding time. He allows no one to come near the back door and, when the door is open, he hangs over the breezy gate to ensure that he will be the first one in. Back at our old ranch, our barn was made of wood and the back door had one small knothole in it about knee high. I would be preparing their dinner, with the door closed, and have the eeriest feeling that I was being watched. I would turn to look at that door and see a mottled Appaloosa eye staring back at me through that knothole. That was more unnerving than entertaining, as it looked so bizarre and creepy. Here, he has carefully managed to slide the two doors apart so that there is just a crack. He presses his eye against the crack to watch us. I love him dearly, but when not expecting it, such actions can unsettle or startle me.

I hollered back through the closed doors that I was hurrying and would be right with him. With that, I dumped the last bucket of feed in Apache's stall, walked to the back, and carefully cracked the sliding doors. Who was standing with his head pressed to the middle of the doors? Ethan, as always.

"Are you ready?" I asked, and a part of me picked up on a gentle nod and smile. The doors were open; the breezy gate was swung out; and as they do every night, they came in the barn in perfect order to eat the dinner that I had labored over in preparation for them. First entered Ethan, then Harley, followed by Apache. Bringing up the rear, was the biggest, youngest, and most fearful, Bart. He feels more comfortable when they are all tucked away in their stalls with their doors closed so that no one can stick their head out and attempt to bite him as he walks down the aisle. He actually stops and looks into each one of their stalls and you can almost hear him say, "Ha, Ha, you can't get me now." Hopefully, one day, he will grow up.

Immediately, the barn was full of the sound of relaxed munching and filled with the sweet odor of horses and feed. I looked back at Kenny, who only bounced two feet instead of three off the pavement. I smiled back and decided to sit down and enjoy this moment. I went into the tack room and pulled out a chair to sit in the center aisle of the barn and commune with the horses. My Brazilian hammock, however, caught my eye. "Ah ha," I cried and snatched up the hammock, this could be good!

Two quick slips of "S" hooks into the installed tie rings on to opposing stalls, and I had the hammock swinging across the center aisle in a heartbeat. Kenny lay down as I eased into the hammock—because he knew that this could be awhile. I sat down with my back propped up and began to swing while singing along with the Christmas music from the radio.

It did not take long to realize that my singing was not appreciated. Bart began to pound on the stall wall with his right front hoof and Apache quit eating to urinate on the clean shavings in the stall, in protest of my singing. I actually was not too offended by Bart's signal to quit, but for Apache to pee in his stall was pushing the envelope a little too far. I felt rather hurt, so I just shut up, closed my eyes, and listened.

The music stirred emotions from seasons long past: seasons of happiness, hope, disappointment, and most recently, pain. But, I am the captain of my own ship and I had no intention to sail into dark and murky waters this night. I simply wanted to let go and feel the companionship of my friends around me. That's when I heard the buzz.

At first, I thought that the radio was slipping off from its frequency, but the music was still there, clearly playing. The buzz was overriding the music. The "white noise" was multi-dimensional and not strictly coming from the tack room. I did not make a serious attempt to think about it as the sounds and smells were like candy to my senses, and the buzz was only the canvas to which the painting of the moment was applied. I relaxed.

I closed my eyes and continued to rock back and forth. There was a feeling of warmth in the barn, while all of those souls were inside eating and enjoying. The buzz, on the other hand, continued to grow. In the beginning, it really was not something to which I was paying much attention; but now I attempted to tune into where it was coming from and what it was. I continued to rock. I could still hear the horses and the music, but now the buzz was growing in volume. As I continued the attempt to identify its source mentally, it was becoming ever more evident that the sound itself was coming from within. It was coming from inside of my head and not relating to anything outside of myself. I was aware that I was humming "Away in the Manger" along with the radio, but it was becoming evident that the white noise also was music. In that music, there were whispers—words, phrases, and thoughts being conveyed. Without knowing it, I gave in to the music from within and opened up to the whispers and words. I heard many voices with varied depths and pitches. Although different, they all blended together in song, and it was soul stirring. I listened and listened and listened, until I finally made out the words that were being sung to me. It came as abruptly and as clearly to me as if a sonic boom had just resonated throughout the barn. In thousands of voices, from deep within my soul, the words being sung in perfect harmony were, "We were there!"

I stopped rocking and the singing stopped; there was total silence. My eyes popped open, and I was looking straight up. Once they focused, I could see two small sparrows in the barn's rafters looking straight down at me. They were looking directly at me with calm assuredness. The radio was silent; only my breathing could be heard. I sat up and looked at the stalls. All of the horses were looking directly at me, calmly, with their heads bowed. I then gazed out across the moonlit pasture and could see the little donkey and her herd of cows staring directly into the lighted barn. Not one of them was moving. I quickly swung around and looked out the other door for Kenny; he was laying calmly with his head between his paws and his big brown eyes staring right at me. I went to stand and, in the silence, the words came again, "We were there!"

I froze.

"We were there that night," the collective voices continued.

"Wait…what…who?" I started to ask.

"Just listen and absorb. Do not ask; we will tell," the voice said. "We were there, in the stable, that night. All of us in one shape or fashion. We were there long before human shepherds and nobles came to see. We were there to see him take his first breath. We were there."

"It is important, at this time, for you to know that we were the selected witnesses, the guardians, and the companions of the Son of the Light. You need to understand that we are closer to the source of goodness and purity than all mankind. You need to know that your fight for our lives is a just and noble one. All of you humans who guard and protect us walk in a very special light. You have now been there, too; now you know; and now you must continue the fight," the voice ended.

"Wait! What do you mean I was there, too?" I called. I stood up and turned around because I did not know to whom I was talking. I looked at the horses, the dog, the birds, the donkey, and the cows. "What do you mean?"

Reality had yet to smack me upside the head as I stared into the horses' eyes. Again, the voice returned, "You were there, too. When you opened your eyes, just a few moments ago, what did you see first?" it asked.

I stammered for a second and came up with, "The birds…
the birds in the barn's rafters."

The voice asked, "What did you see next?"

"Well," I said, "I saw the horses looking at me from their
stalls. The donkey, the cows, and Kenny the bouncing dog were
looking at me."

"Yes," the voice said. "And what were the first impressions
in the life of the Gifted One when he first opened up his eyes
in that stable long, long, long ago?"

"I would imagine that when he first opened his eyes, lying
in a manager, he saw the rafters in the barn ceiling with the
birds looking down—" I stopped talking so quickly that I
almost bit my tongue. There was a warm sensation washing
over me, and it was more than just the tie-in and realization of
what had just occurred.

I could not speak and was about to sit back down when the
voice added, "Yes, you see now. You have been there too. We
all have been there, yet, few humans can remember. This is our
gift to you. Carry the light and chase the darkness. We love all
of you for what you do."

In hearing those words, there was something else that I could not then, nor can I now, describe. Perhaps a sigh, perhaps it was a catch as if emotion had welled up, but there was something there, not spoken, that touched me more than the words.

In a dreamlike state of numbness, I began the process of releasing the horses from their stalls to their pasture—this was done in the exact reverse of the entry process. I moved like a robot, as the power of the words and the moment were still within me. I opened up Ethan's stall, and he walked out and stood in the middle of the back door, as he often does.

Harley was next. I stood at his stall door and allowed my hand to move down his furry side as he calmly walked by me and out past Ethan.

Apache usually flattens his ears, when he sees Ethan in the doorway, and chases him out, but not tonight. When I opened up his stall, he calmly walked past us both without any notice.

Finally, Bart was freed to return to the beloved round bale. As he exited, I asked him to stop, and I gave him a hug. He gently kissed my bald spot and headed out past Ethan.

I then turned my attention to Ethan. I stood next to him in the doorway and gazed out upon what he was viewing. The donkey and cows had gone back to grazing in the moonlight and the neighbor's horses were tucked away in their barn with their heads hanging out. Our three were all drinking from the trough, together, and the sky was fantastic with the moon and stars. It was picture, postcard perfect.

As he stood next to me, I put my hand on Ethan's withers. He turned to me and put his left nostril right against my heart, which placed his left eye at the same level with mine. I said, "Merry Christmas, my friend." He blinked, turned, and then stepped out into the night. As I watched that big Appaloosa butt dwindle from the light of the barn, he stopped and turned. Regardless of what anyone says, he had the biggest smile on his face that any horse could have.

I lowered my head, pulled my glasses off to wipe the tears off the lenses, closed the back door, turned off the lights, walked out of the barn, and stood over Kenny, who still had not budged. "Want to go inside, boy?" He bounced five feet high this time, and we dribbled each other up the driveway and to the house like we were two ten-year-old kids headed for a game of basketball. The moon cast shadows of us dancing on our way as the horses continued to hum in the pasture, "We were there."

A TALE OF TWO HERDS

Out west, in the dusty state of Nevada, lived several loose-knit herds of wild horses. Being horses, they preferred to be in numbers. For many years, their herds were undefined, and they drifted here and there. Then the attack started.

Men on horses and machines began to pursue them, to drive them into holding pens and cart them off to places where horses never returned. There was panic, strife, and great sadness running deep within the horse nation. They were confused, disjointed, and not of one mind. The more confused they became, the easier prey they were to those who hunted them.

One old stallion standing on a bluff overlooking the valley at the setting of the sun had a vision. He had seen a lot in his life. He had loved many mares and sired many foals and, for that reason, he knew he had to act to save all of the horses that dotted the floor of the valley beneath him. He had a vision of building a great herd: a herd with the strength to take care of the weak and frail; a herd that would close ranks and defend off all attackers; a herd that would actually turn and fight rather than lie down and die for those who chased them; a herd filled with love, compassion, and accountability.

He sighed and walked gently through the growing darkness to gather his forces and build such a herd. A new spark of life had been lit in his soul, and for the first time, in many moons, he was aware that mares surrounded him. This could be difficult.

Meanwhile, on the other side of the valley, lived a very young mare. She considered herself boss mare, years before her time, and for that, many other mares respected her for her determination. She needed experience, so they joined her herd. Even though inexperienced, she did a good job of surrounding herself with those who knew how to manage, protect, and act as a mother and advisor when she was lost. She had a knack for attracting such mares and even managed to attract the brother of the old stallion. Her herd grew and grew, and this pleased the young mare.

Often, she would slip across the valley floor and visit the old stallion on the other side to seek his advice. In fact, this became a standard practice. The old stallion did not resent these visits, as he looked upon her as if he had sired her. As time passed, he became proud of her. Occasionally, he would inquire as to the status of his brother and once assured that all was well, would go back to grazing. Most of the skills the inexperienced mare had were based upon the old stallion's leadership and advice.

As time passed and the herds grew, the old stallion's brother began to cross the valley floor to visit with his sibling. They would chat and speak of life. The old stallion asked his brother to join his herd, but the younger stallion always returned to the other side of the valley with very little explanation outside of the fact that he was very comfortable and trusted the senior mares in the herd. He respected them greatly, and they were good friends.

There were many attacks on the herds. When the old stallion's herd would come under attack, he would either lead them off to safety to survive another day or stand and fight. He picked his battles wisely. However, when the young mare's herd would come under attack she would run off, alone, and leave the herd to fend for themselves. Soon they learned to be quick on their feet, work together, and not to count on the young mare for guidance. This process continued to fester until the entire group of lead mares was ready to leave the herd and go off to greener pastures.

This troubled the younger stallion and several of the mares to the point that they went to speak with the old stallion. They came to him for help as they felt their entire life process was crumbling and the herd they loved was dissolving. The mares were very upset. In fact, they pushed and shoved the younger brother along. They wanted him to speak and plead their case since they were not happy horses.

They reached the other side of the valley and approached the wise old stallion where he quietly listened to their story of loss and pain. As he hushed them, he called over several of his most trusted boss mares. The visiting company continued with their heartbreaking plea for help, and all pulled in closely to share ideas. The concept of joining the separate herds into one was born. They would have twice the defense, twice the number of eyes, and twice the ability to fight back. They could not conceive of any horse objecting to this plan. It was win-win.

The old stallion went to discuss this with his herd, while the young mare's group went off to speak with her. They were so excited that they did not walk. They galloped across the valley floor with their manes flying and their tails trailing. The young stallion was having difficulty keeping up. Granted, he was the younger brother of the old stallion, but he was many years older than these mares. Nonetheless, he gave it a great show and followed from behind, breathing their dust and loving the scent of their excitement. They had hope. They had a future.

When they reached their herd, they attempted to locate the young mare leader. As usual, she was nowhere to be found. They even sent out scouts, but she appeared to have taken flight. They were worried, fretful, as they wanted to speak with her and bond the two herds together. She was not among the other horses, so their excitement waned, and they anxiously awaited her return. Then it happened. The attack commenced.

Out of the sky, from the west and coming up the valley, were helicopters—lots of them. They were just a few feet from the valley's floor. Out of the hills, following closely behind, poured horses with men on their backs firing guns. The herd had never seen this in such force and froze in place until one of the mares screamed, "Run, join the old stallion's herd. There is safety in numbers and we must run for our lives and pray for leadership." The senior mares and the young stallion reared, pawing at the air, and bolted for the other side of the valley.

The herd stood frozen. One by one, they looked after the bolting leaders and began to follow, looking over their shoulders, and running for all they were worth. They were joining the other herd and running for their lives. One by one, two by two they turned and followed the dust trail to the other side of the valley while the hunters drew closer. They ran for safety, leadership, and protection.

As they ran, they all knew in their hearts that they were doing the right thing—heading toward sanctuary and safety. They all knew. But, being horses, they could not articulate their feelings. Nonetheless, they knew they were going to be safe.

Then, out of the blue storming up over the bluff, came the inexperienced mare. She must have been grazing in the center of the valley just out of sight of both herds. Charging directly at the lead horses, which were frantically running towards safety, she screamed that they had no right to lead "her" herd. She accused the senior mares and the stallion of stealing her herd and emphatically denied their unity. In her uncontrollable rage, she demanded the majority to turn and run back—right into the hands of the hunters.

Her attack was so savage and startling that as she ran through the lead horses kicking furiously at the mares, her gnashing teeth left a deep gash down the young stallion's side. Her immature actions only convinced the leaders to run harder and move faster. Sadly, several of the mares in the herd faltered and one or two stumbled. As the leaders ran for safety, one of the older boss mares peeled off to follow the young mare. The mature mare joined in the attack, while several other confused horses turned to join them. They joined not so much out of support but more out of fear of the unknown. They followed the inexperienced mare as she tore apart and tried to kill the herd that she had worked so hard to build.

The herd ran on. As they approached the old stallion's herd, they noted that the other herd was drawn up into a tight circle with the old stallion standing outside. The walls of the circle opened and the new herd ran in, only to be enclosed by the old stallion's group. It was a quiet moment. The mares that formed the circle turned one by one and welcomed the new herd, promptly turning around to protect the new additions. The old stallion came inside to welcome them, winked at his bloodied brother, and told him that he was due for a few battle scars. He then muscled his way back through the circle to view the spectacle that was taking place on the other side of the valley floor.

The mares greeted each other and bonded while some of the new herd actually muscled up to the circle to be a part of the defensive perimeter. The young stallion pushed his way back through the circle of mares to join his brother in protecting the "new" herd. The nasty gash on his side ran red with blood, but the warm flow down his side gave him a feeling of accomplishment. He knew it would be okay since it was the right thing to do. While he walked up to his brother, he noted that he was, not only followed, but also preceded by the bulk of head mares from the combined herds. They formed their own knot of comradeship outside the circle of defense and then stopped and watched the senseless, stupid drama unfold across the desert's floor.

Across the valley, the young, inexperienced mare screamed to the herd to follow her. She told them that it would be okay and that all was well. Even when the first lasso fell over her neck, she did not cease. The mares that followed her screamed in panic. Suddenly, they knew they had been betrayed. They knew it was a mistake. They ran to and fro only to be roped and thrown into waiting trailers. The mature mare, who had given her all for the herd, just stopped. She stood still, hung her head, looked back towards the others, and cried. She offered no resistance as she was roped and lead away to her doom. As the trailers pulled away, the old stallion, his brother, and the mares could hear the inexperienced mare screaming that she was in charge, all was fine, she was the boss mare, and how could they defy her. Her voice disappeared long before the dust settled from the trailers upon the valley floor.

As the knot of horse leaders watched, there were no tears, though sadness touched their hearts. The old stallion turned his head to look back at the herd behind them and softly whispered, "We owe them the future. Today is the past. We need to move forward and protect them."

The lead mares nodded in approval.

The stallion's brother added, "I know of a really great green pasture just over that hill."

The old stallion snorted, "Yeah, right. Lick your wounds and behave."

The mares nickered while the brothers' eyes went half-lidded and the group of them walked back to the new herd to form a plan and live yet another day. Life would go on; the herd would survive; and the drama would cease.

ON SLEEPING WITH HORSES

I had been home from the office for only an hour, yet the rain meter had gained another inch on the gauge. It was unbelievable. It was cold, dark, windy, and way too wet. There were white caps moving in the pastures and the horses must have been huddled up on the south end of the barn, under cover, and wondering why I had not yet let them in. It was time to get moving.

Dashing out the back door, down under the eaves of the garages in an effort to stay dry, I made a hard left and sprinted towards the barn, attempting to limit my exposure to the downpour. The wind was out of the north; so, as I slid the door open, a bucket or two of cold icy rain followed me into the barn. I punched the light switch "on" and could not believe the ruckus of noise that surrounded me once inside. A deluge of rain on the multiple metal roofs of a barn with porches was mind-numbing. I went to the tack room to turn up the radio, but to no avail. It was still too noisy. So, I headed to the leeward south end to open up the doors and look for the horses.

I didn't have to look too far as there the four of them stood, side-by-side, under the extended roof in the dry sand: wet, forlorn, hungry, and urgent. In unison, they snorted, "*Let us in!*" Promptly, I obliged.

This was easy tonight, as Terry had already been out to clean their stalls and add the appropriate amount of feed pellets and rice bran to each stall's feed bin. The stall doors were already open, so being the intelligent horses that they are, the four wet horses promptly shuffled into their respective stalls.

I had no intention of letting them back out into the weather, so I closed up the barn doors, locked all of their stall doors, and swung open each of the barred Dutch door top halves so that they could hang their heads out and converse with one another. They had fresh buckets of water hanging, but I needed to add several flakes of hay to each of their hay mangers. I hated to do that while they were eating, as the hayracks are right over their food bowls, so I opted to wait.

I was freezing, but thought that it would be nice to move a chair out into the center aisle and listen to the rain while they ate. But, once again in the tack room, the allure of my Brazilian hammock caught my eye and captured my heart. I remembered the last time I had used that hammock while the horses ate, and it warmed my heart. I would use it again tonight like a comfortable magic carpet that would take me to places I had never been. I quickly snapped it into place, climbed into it, letting it wrap up around me like a cocoon, and pulled my collar up around my ears in a feeble attempt to stay warm. Mmmmm. It was cold, but comfortable.

I just rested. I could not hear the horses eating over the din of rain on tin, but it felt relaxing swinging in the hammock while the horses ate. The tension of the day slowly seeped out of me. It made me feel warm from the inside out, instead of the other way around.

It was only a matter of minutes, while I lay there turning off the switches of human sensibilities, before I was keenly aware that I was being watched. Actually, I could hear several urgent nickers over the sound of the rain. When I opened up my eyes, four distinctly different horse heads were gazing at me. Their expressions made me smile; their looks were so easy to read.

Bart: "What are you doing in here?"

Harley: "I am glad you are in here; you need to be here more often."

Ethan: "I feel safe with you in here!"

Apache: "When do I get some hay?"

So, I installed the flakes through their feed doors and stood back to look at them as they ate, and, in turn, they glanced back at me while they did so. The contentment was there, their eyes half-lidded as the hay meant warmth and pleasure to their equine bellies. Their pleasure caused me to sit in the hammock and hang in their equine world for a moment longer. I closed my eyes, hung my head, and thanked whomever or whatever was responsible for allowing me this precious moment that I was so blessed to share.

Plus it was warm, warm from within. I could feel the horses' contentment, their happiness at the simplest of pleasures, and the pure state of being in tune with each other and their surroundings. As I allowed this contentment to wash over me, I saw in my mind's eye the sun shining on a green, rolling pasture. I was running—running as fast as the wind. My heart was pounding with excitement, not from the running, but from the vision of a beautiful mare scampering just a few yards ahead of me. Her mane was flying in the wind with her head turned back to see if I was following, there was a beguiling smile on her lips. The curve of her rump compelled me and the lift of her tail was entrancing. I shook my head and cleared my mind; I was warm and glowing. Three of the four horses were not paying attention to me, but the fourth, Apache, had a glint in his eye as he watched me from his stall. I looked closer and could swear that he winked before he went back to eating.

I left the hammock hanging, said my goodbyes, turned off the light, and made up my mind that the following night I would be prepared to stay. I would stay the night to find out and experience the end of that little tale, and I would dream with my friends the dreams that they dreamt. I would allow my spirit to fly across the fields with them, to feel the wind in my mane, the thunder in my hooves, and the heart pounding in my chest. The little mare? Well, we shall see. I promised to see my adventure through and, tomorrow, I would sleep with the horses.

AN ANGEL IN COWBOY BOOTS

It was almost exactly one year ago that I sat next to my mother's hospital bed and watched her life light slowly dim. Perhaps it is not always healthy to reflect upon such painful memories and attempt to put the pieces of the puzzle in place. No matter how hard you struggle, you just cannot make them all fit. While the images and words from that painful period float through my mind like wisps of fog, I have come to realize that there are several tales intertwined within that singular story. Events occurred during that time that seemed trivial or of limited importance. But, as the dust settles and the big picture comes into focus, I see several shining parables with incredible clarity. I am amazed that they slipped through my fingers at the time, but on the other hand, I am thankful that I can see them now. It is like dessert or finding an Easter egg: something special, something you did not expect, and something, now, to share.

On the last day that I spent with my mother, I had great success in getting her moved from the hospital to a rehabilitation facility. My main mission was to get her out of that building full of sick people and into an area where perhaps she could be made to feel better, to have a chance at life, and, in so doing, to survive. Once she was all tucked in and asleep, I knew that after being there for nearly a week, my primary mission had finally been accomplished. I now needed to make plans to return home to my wife and four-legged children back in Louisiana. It had been a long week spent in Florida; however, I did have one last task to accomplish, and, with mom resting peacefully, I headed out the door.

Thirty-some miles away from Citrus Springs is Ocala, Florida. Ocala is a small yet bustling metropolis, and within that quaint little town, my in-laws resided. I decided to head the big red dually in that direction and began calling them, only to no avail. I had been in Florida almost a week and had not seen them due to the time I had spent with my mother, so I thought I would grab a chance this last afternoon. I continued heading in that direction, through the rolling countryside dotted with herds of Thoroughbreds and large oak trees. I kept on, as there were other things that I could do while I awaited for them to arrive home

I made it into Ocala still with no contact with my in-laws. I stopped at Stateline Tack for some horse goodies and the toy that I was seeking for my mom. As luck would have it, I found a happy, floppy, little horse doll that looked just like our own Harley, the Happy Rescue Horse. I took it with me.

After shopping and no contact with Mom and Dad Z, it was well past lunch and I was famished. I headed up the road to a local Micro Brew Pub for a bite to eat and some samplings of their own fresh brewed beer. I could use the break.

I pulled into the pub's parking lot and spent a moment or two selecting a "safe" place to park. As anyone who drives a large truck knows, it is all too easy to get "hemmed" into a parking spot if you do not plan ahead for an adequate escape route. I rolled around for a bit until I found one that would suffice in the back. I went inside and settled down on a barstool with cell phone in hand to make yet another call to Terry's parents—still no luck.

I asked for a lunch menu and ordered one of their light pilsners, right up front, as I was planning on going on a little bit of a taste testing tour. I had some time to spend, and I loved this place. I just needed to decompress and let some of the tension and sadness leak out of my pores before I went back to say goodbye to my mother.

I took the first sip of my beer and closely examined it in the glass. As I let it linger on my tongue for a moment, I gently and slowly tipped my mug from side to side to watch the performance of the beer's head on the side of the glass. It left lacelike patterns. I smiled—good sign. I swallowed the first mouthful and a fresh feeling of bittersweet hops washed across my tongue. "Ahh," I sighed, "it's good." Given that I brew my own beer, I'm not only very particular, but I also take great pride in what I create. My brew is a work of love, and sharing it with family and friends is one of the highest compliments that

I can pay to them, at least in my twisted brew master's mind. As I watched the carbonated bubbles stream from the bottom of the mug to the top I noticed that someone had come inside and leaned over the bar to ask the bartender a question. The bartender nodded and promptly headed over in my direction. The bartender asked if I owned a red Dodge dually with out-of-state tags that read RESQHRS (pronounced Rescue Horse). "That would be me; is there a problem?" I replied.

The stranger then stepped up and said that he just wanted to verify whose truck that was outside in the lot. When I confirmed that it was mine, I asked his intent.

"Nothing in particular, my friend. I was just curious as it caught my eye with the horse graphics on the side and the tag and all. Being a horseman, I knew that the owner was involved with horses, too, and I just preferred to share a drink with a fellow believer than with a stranger," he said.

"I *am* a stranger," I countered.

"No, you're not," he said and promptly ordered a Jack Black straight up.

While he spoke with the bartender and eased on to the barstool beside me, I sized him up. He had on western boots, weathered with a bit of caked-on mud and dust; jeans, slightly soiled and stained by grass, just like an honest, working farmhand's; work-style leather belt, with a simple western buckle; a western cut denim shirt; and a baseball cap with a horse's head to finish out the ensemble. When he turned back to me, I studied his build and face: fit and muscular; about six feet; ruddy completion; light reddish-blond hair; clean-shaven, except for the late afternoon shadow that was starting to appear; and no glasses. I dipped my head to gaze under his visor only to see bright green eyes and bushy blonde eyebrows. Eyebrows— now that bothered me, as those who have none always covet those who have plenty. With the cap on, I could not tell if he had a full head of hair or not; my ego told me it was probably better to leave that issue alone.

"So, where are you from?" he asked with a big smile.

"Lafayette, Louisiana," I stated and quickly asked, "How about you?" I was uncomfortable launching off into an immediate discussion about my vitals and background with a total stranger whom I had not even known for more than ten brief seconds.

The bartender brought over his shot of Jack Black, and with a well-orchestrated toss of the hand and jerk of the head, the sour mash disappeared between his lips. "Ahhh...mmm...

Lexington, Kentucky," he sighed, as he obviously enjoyed his drink. "Home of fast women and beautiful horses," he laughed.

"I think that you have that twisted around a tad," I snickered.

He smiled and slapped me on my back. "Depends upon your perspective, my friend; it's all a matter of perception." He allowed his hand on my back to linger one brief second before he gave me a parting blow and removed it. For that one solitary second, I felt a connection, a kindred bonding of a spirit that mirrored mine. My level of interest jumped a few notches while my pain and resistance started to melt; I warmed to his company.

"What brings you to the bustling metropolis of Ocala, Florida?" I inquired. I deliberately mispronounced Ocala to sound like Oh-Ka-La, kind of a local joke.

He caught it and snorted, "I like that better," and pointed at me and winked. "Another?"

I nodded and added to the bartender, "Let me try one of your wheat brews. We are going on a taste tour this afternoon." And, with that, I received another slap on the back.

My new friend told me that he trains horses. When things are too cold in Kentucky, he comes down to Ocala and works with managing a barn and training until the weather warms up enough for him to head back home. I asked of his family. He said they stayed up north while he lives out of the quarters of his horse trailer for the winter. We chatted and drank on while he talked to me about natural horsemanship and his relationship with horses. He spoke of how a real trainer feels his horses and knows their needs. He spoke of love, partnership, insight, and consistency.

I listened while I graduated from the wheat, to a red, to ale, to something that now escapes me. He kept hitting those JD shots, slapping me on the back, and speaking of the spirituality of the horse and the respect he feels for members of the horse nation. I became lost in his words; I tuned out what was around me. It never occurred to me that I was not talking, nor was I even participating in this conversation, I was only listening.

It is not natural for me to sit with my mouth shut, particularly if adult beverages are in abundant supply. Nonetheless, I remember being mesmerized by his stories of contact, of listening, of feeling, of challenging, and making a difference. I could hear my heart race when he spoke of laying his hand on a horse's withers, bowing his head, and projecting a feeling of love and a vision of him stroking the horse. And, as his head was bowed, he could feel that gentle, warm breath in his left ear and a gentle nuzzle to the side of his head. The world was gone to me now; the last week of watching all the suffering and sadness was a lifetime away. I felt uplifted, invigorated, and awed while I just sat there and listened.

Alas, just when I felt as if I might slip over to the other side, I felt a strong slap on the back and heard the words, "Time to get after it, my friend; you and I both have things that we need to get done. My job is easier than yours." And, with that, he stood up, I shook my head, tuned the real world back in, and fumbled for my wallet. "Your money isn't any good here, this one's on me. It's a small world; you can buy me the next round when we meet up again." Flustered and a little groggy from the world tour of microbrews, I nodded my head in thanks.

I tried to look at my watch as we moseyed outside into the sunshine and headed towards my truck. My eyes were too blurry to make out the hands of the watch. However, the sun was still up, which was a good sign.

He accompanied me over to the truck; I unlocked the door; he shook my hand and gestured to the door. I climbed in and rolled down the window. The smiling stranger kindly rested both of his hands on my arm, which was positioned on the window sill, and then leaned purposely into my space. "I won't lie to you my friend," he said in a very steady and calm voice, "It won't be okay; it will not be easy; and it will hurt like nothing you have ever felt." He paused and smiled, "But they are there and you are not alone. They are there, if only you listen. Just stop and listen to the horses." He then abruptly stepped back, squeezed and released my arm, nodded, touched the brim of his cap, spun on his heel and briskly walked down the sidewalk and made a quick turn around the building.

Confused, I fired up the truck, backed up, and wheeled around the lot to where he had just disappeared. Although feeling a vague sense of relief, I did not understand what had just happened. As I rounded the building, I searched both the walk and the lot for the stranger who had just left my side. I stopped the truck and waited for another vehicle to move as he could not have walked to one, started it up, backed out, and then driven away in the brief seconds since he left me. I sat there watching and thinking, but nothing moved. I took a few more breaths and still nothing stirred. I sat in contemplation: I had not asked his name, nor had he mine. I never opened my mouth; he knew nothing of my life or me; I shared nothing. What was he talking about; what was going on; who was that horseman from Kentucky?

As the seconds turned into minutes, I had the sensation that a strange and unusual feeling of peace was washing over me. I felt that there was no need to worry, no need to question, no need to fret; just go and do the job that I had to do. I needed to go about my business, take the stuffed Harley horse to my mother, and say goodbye, for the last time, ever.

A wry smile crept up to my lips and a sigh softly escaped me as I put the truck in gear and drove away, never to think of that stranger again—until today.

THE DRIVE-BY

Once upon a time, on a small one-acre paddock in rural central Texas, there resided several horses, unfortunately, not in the best of conditions. It was a mean enclosure, boarded with barbed wire and natural cut poles, whose bark had been eaten off long ago by the horses held captive within.

There was no grass left. There were only rocks, litter, junk, and dung. In the southwest corner was the old rusting shell of a 1971 Super Beetle—a proud car in its day—now diminished to a rust red hulk with broken shards for windows that looked like the ragged teeth of a dinosaur long dead. Nearby, several faded and broken plastic tubs littered the area, some overturned, others shattered. These vessels once held life-giving water and feed; their present condition indicated that such memories were in a distant past.

In the southeast corner, stretched out like a toppled skeleton of a giant alien, was a ruined windmill. It had come crashing down during a thunderstorm quite some time ago. Its broken vanes lay very close to the barbed wire fence. Only a few more feet and the prisoners within the enclosure could have escaped; but that was not their fate. The windmill lay ruined, no longer able to provide the captive horses with the water that they so desperately needed.

Near the northwest corner, stood an emaciated gelding that shivered from pain. He made no sound, but simply rocked from front to back. It was obvious that he was in severe agony. Besides the protruding bones, there was a gunshot wound to his left rear hip where dried bloodstains ran down his back leg. Black flies still swarmed around the dried up wound and one could see maggots moving within. The stench was unbearable. He stared off towards the horizon, his pained mind seeing vistas not visible to the naked eye. His breathing was labored, dry, and raspy. His eyes were glazed and sunken from starvation. He hoped for the pain to stop, he hoped for release, he hoped for freedom.

The eastern portion of the mean paddock fronted a secondary gravel road, not often traveled. When people drove by, no one stopped to help or even bothered to slow down. As a rule, people threw beer bottles or cans and fired guns at the horses from time to time. One bullet even found a home in the left hip of the starving gelding.

In the middle of the death cell laid a gasping mare; above her stood a grotesquely thin stallion and another mare in just as bad of shape. Their breed and color where indistinguishable due to their lack of form and soiled, patchy, coats. Their heads were lowered as they looked intently at the ailing mare.

"What did I do?" whispered the mare, "What did I do? I loved them, loved them all who came into my life." She paused to cough painfully, "What did I do to deserve this?" She sighed and the sound of her breath rattled from deep down in her throat. She wheezed and coughed again. "I loved my people so..." The two other horses could see that she mouthed the word "much" as another rattle escaped from her. But this one lasted longer and when it stopped, there was not another. Her eyes no longer blinked.

The mare and the stallion lowered their heads to nudge her, but there was no movement. Slowly, they backed away with their heads still low and their eyes half closed. They stopped some distance away and looked at each other, sighed, and then looked over at the wounded gelding shivering in the corner. The stallion shook his head. He was about to speak when they heard a sound behind them on the frontage road.

Slowly and carefully, the two starving horses turned to find that a vehicle had stopped on the road and someone was peering out of the driver's window at them. They did not see many people and had not seen anyone stop for a long time, so they gave the vehicle their full attention. It was a small pick-up truck. Inside, they could see a female human staring at them. A little light went on in both of their heads, and they were drawn to come closer.

As they slowly and painfully shuffled towards the fence, the woman fiddled around the inside of the truck, popped open the door, and jumped out with a camera in her right hand. She left the truck door open and began to snap pictures of the horses. The horses saw the camera, but they were not afraid. For a fleeting moment, they hoped that the camera was something to eat. So, when they reached the fence, they hung their heads over and beseeched the woman to come closer.

The woman carefully walked across the road's shoulder, picked her way through the trash in the ditch, and came up to the fence line. She stood several feet away from the horses and continued to take pictures. She had been so busy taking pictures that the horses had yet to see her face.

Finally, the mechanical clicking stopped and the woman lowered the camera revealing a tear-smeared face and downturn lips with very small sobs escaping from her mouth. She stood there for a moment while the tears streamed and looked disbelievingly at the horses. The stallion cocked his head as he looked at her, and a gentle little laugh escaped the smile that popped up on her face. She slowly walked up to both of them and lovingly stroked their heads. They attempted to see if she had food, but she had none—only words.

The woman whispered, "Hold on babies, I will get help. Don't give in, fight. I will get help." And, with that, she bolted across the ditch, up the shoulder, and jumped into her truck. She rolled down the window and hollered, "I'll be back. Hang in there. I'll be back!" Before the words could fade, the truck leaped forward in a cloud of dust, spewing loose gravel in all directions. Soon, all that was left was a settling cloud of dust drifting across the enclosure.

The stallion turned to look over the mare in the direction the truck that had disappeared. He laid his chin on her withers and sighed when he heard yet another sound: the crunch of gravel, behind them, and a dull hollow thud.

They turned to see that the gelding had gone down; he had fallen on his right side with his head hung up on the bottom strand of the barbed wire fence. With what little strength they had left, they turned and moved as fast as they could towards the gasping gelding. As they drew nearer, they could hear his moans and the mantra to which they had all become accustomed. They could hear him articulate, "What did I do? What did I do? I loved them and gave them my all!"

The stallion stopped; the mare attempted to do so, also, and almost stumbled. They stood a short distance from the gelding, listening to his song of lament. The stallion slowly turned his head to look down the road at the now long-departed truck. The mare followed his gaze.

"I hope she hurries," he coughed.

"I hope that she does not forget." The mare nodded.

They both stood there, shaking and rocking, and...they waited.

THE NEAR MISS

She was driving north, up that old country road that lead to her elderly aunt's house. This was a trip that she'd made hundreds of times over the past several decades. She headed straight up north, on the old gravel road, while kicking up enough dust to be seen by the space shuttle as it soared over Texas. As she embraced that thought, it pressed her to move even faster, as if to say hello to those up in space. Maybe that was why she had never seen them; she did not know.

Today was different though. For no reason, as she raced up that empty country road, she paid attention to the often barren and always empty country land. Her eyes drifted from left to right as she tapped her left foot to the rhythm of the Blood, Sweat, and Tears' song booming out of her XM radio, which permanently locked on the 1970s station. She swayed her head from side to side to match the flow of the music and allowed her mind to drift back to the "good old days" when her heart was pure, whole, intact, and ready to take on the world. A lifetime away, this used to be "their" song. She remembered the words he used to woo her with as they sat looking out at the dark lake, at midnight, in his dad's new Dodge Polaris. This song was playing on the car's radio that night. She allowed herself to remember the kiss, the caress, and the feeling of her heart leaping out of her chest, and just as she was slipping down the tunnel of darkness towards remembering the betrayal, she saw them.

She jumped and clutched the steering wheel as if electrocuted, and snapped her head around to the left as she gasped in horror at what she saw. It took several seconds for her body to react to what her eyes had just seen, so her truck continued to barrel up the road until her shaking foot finally found the strength to step on the brake pedal. Stones scattered as she came to a half-controlled skid in the middle of that desolate country road. She sat there for a minute, softly panting and trying to put the image into perspective. She had traveled too far out of range and could no longer view the horror. What were they? How hideous! What could they be?

Being alone, she thought that maybe it would be better to continue and not go back. Perhaps it would be best if she just continued to head up the road to her aunt's house where they would sip diet sodas and she would hear the same old stories about her deceased mother—good stories, but old after you had heard them at least a thousand times. Maybe that should be what she should do, but she would never be able to relax, as the images would be haunting her during her visit. She knew that she would have to drive by them on the way home—in the dark. What to do?

While her mind debated over the best course of action to take, her heart put the truck in gear, backed it up, turned it around, and headed back down the road to the location of the viewing. Once there, the truck deftly performed a U-turn and parked on the other side of the road with the driver's side window in full view of the scene from hell. She slipped the truck into park, pushed on the parking brake, let it idle to keep the AC running, took a deep breath, and turned her head to the left to stare out over the shoulder and the barbed wire fence beyond. A little gasp was heard as she quickly drew air into her lungs, her lower teeth slowly applied pressure to her upper lip, and the tears that began to form in her eyes made the vision of death and dying begin to blur and appear surreal.

As she sat frozen, with her head twisted to the left, her right hand appeared to develop an intelligence of its own and without any visual direction from the head, it began searching and groping on the front bench seat, looking for something. It rifled through the newspaper; bypassed the purse; and bingo, snatched a hold of the handle of the digital camera that was lying close to the passenger's side. The right hand and arm pulled it close to her chest as the left hand rolled down the window; little whimpers of despair filled the cab. As the driver's window clunked itself down into the cradle inside the door, a blast of hot air roared into the cab bringing the stench of death, of rotting flesh and entrails. She almost vomited in the truck, but pressed her left hand to her mouth as her right hand and camera shook against her chest. She wept.

Through the tears, she found the strength to put the camera to her face, to focus the telephoto lens and begin clicking off pictures. She cried as the clarity of the horror came to her through the viewfinder; her heart was breaking and she felt so helpless. As she sat and clicked the pictures, two of the horrible, emaciated skeletons turned to look at her. They had been standing over the body of one of their own, in a swarm of black flies, but they must have heard her. Awkwardly, they turned to face her, some several dozen yards away. They turned and stared with sunken dull eyes, eyes that screamed with pain, fear, confusion, and abandonment. They stared, and she took pictures. The larger one tried to move towards her and almost fell as he stumbled on the rocks; the smaller one tried to follow but had to stop every other step to work up the strength to move forward. For what seemed like hours, they painfully stumbled their way towards the fence that ran along the road and closer to her, as she still took pictures. They finally made it to the fence. It appeared to be a serious test of their endurance, and they hung their heads over the barbed wire and panted while they watched her. Off in the far corner she could see another one standing, rocking in pain, but he did not turn, he did not move; only these two came and they looked directly at her.

She felt the pull. She could almost touch the feelings that these two exuded, and she knew that she must, at the very least, go to them. As she opened the door of the truck and stumbled across the road and through the ditch, she frantically continued snapping pictures. The stench was increasingly unbearable as she got closer to the emaciated, fly-covered beings. She stopped pushing on the shutter button, lowered the camera, and tried a weak attempt at a smile so as not to frighten them. Instead of a sob, a frustrated squeak of a laugh came from her lips. The two looked so intently at her as if she could save them from the fate that had befallen them, as well as those behind them in the mean paddock. She felt weak and helpless, and slowly reached out to touch them. Two sore covered noses stretched out to smell her hand in hopes that she had brought them nourishment. But, all she could do was stroke their patchy, scabbed foreheads and whisper, "Hold on babies, I will get help. Don't give in. Fight! I promise I will get help." With that, she bolted down the ditch, up the shoulder, across the road, and hopped back into her truck. She rolled down the window and hollered, "I'll be back. Hang in there; I'll be back!" Before the words could fade, she pushed on the accelerator and the truck leaped forward in a flurry of flying gravel and dust.

Her pulse was pounding and her mind was racing. She had to help; she had to do something—they were about to die. She must take action. As she drove to the sanctuary of her aunt's home where a phone and a computer waited, she began to form the plan: a direction of actions that could be taken, the numbers that she needed to call, and the Website she needed to visit. She would not wait; she would not stop; she needed to save those poor horses.

As she drove out of sight, another equine soul departed the world in the mean paddock behind her. She did not know this nor did she need to. She had given a gift to the two who remained, the two that were still prisoners in their cell. She had left a bit of herself with them; she had given them hope. As the dust began to settle from her rapid exit, the two who remained looked in her direction with dulling eyes, yet uplifted hearts. They knew, their equine spirits knew. They knew that they had a chance. There might be hope because they knew, in their heart of hearts, that a Horse Rescuer had been born that day. They knew, and so, they waited.

WHISPERS IN THE NIGHT

I've been gone for several weeks, on the road, doing human things and attempting to meet the demands of others' needs. In traveling about, we are surrounded and assailed by all that is human: the machines, the noise, the people, and the unnatural mechanical buzzing that gnaws at the brain just underneath our consciousness. It wears one out and deflates the soul, leaving only emptiness. So, I welcomed coming home.

Although the commotion does not cease by being here, I can steal several moments of quiet and reflection with the horses and attempt to bring the universe back into balance. In fact, as I write, the sun is just pushing up over the tree line in the northeast and its rays are setting afire the low mist that has drifted into our pastures from the corn fields. I can actually sit here and see the silhouettes of five large backs, bodies hidden by the mist, slowly moving in the east pasture. They look like the smooth backs of a pod of pilot whales, gently swimming through a channel to the sea. Occasionally, a head surfaces as if to both take in air and to check out what is happening in the world above, and then back to grazing, drifting in the mist of the early dawn. Just seeing this and sharing it has pumped some life back into my spirit.

Last night, after our houseguests were off to their quarters and gently asleep, and Terry had been zoned out for quite some time, I quietly slipped out of the house and jumped the pasture fence. I wanted a moment alone with the guys and, true to form, all grazing ceased. Heads were raised in momentary alarm, but a few quiet whispers from me put them back at ease so that the five of them returned to grazing. Actually, they returned with even more gusto than before, as the rule is that they can relax their guard when I am in the pasture. I will take over guard duty, and they can then devote 100% of their time to eating.

I have learned not to force thought, idea, or suggestions upon them at times like this. In the dark, it is best to go from one to another, gently stroking and scratching, and occasionally reaching down to tear off some grass as if I am grazing, too. This seems to relax them further. Once they were comfortable with me grazing amongst them, I listened; I closed my eyes, leaned up against Ethan, and turned off my mind.

I was both shocked and pleased with what I heard, as this is no story of words of wisdom coming from my equine companions; instead, it is a note on happiness. As I stood there, I could hear humming: a distant but stirring tune being hummed by those around me, and perhaps overtones from others far away. I heard no words, no verse, no refrain; just a spiritually soft stream of gentle and contented humming that touched my heart. Although no words were apparent, the meaning was clear. It was clear enough even for an aging human to discern. The humming was a song of hope, of happy things to come, a tune of love and outreach, and most of all, a song of forgiveness.

I pressed my ear against Ethan's hairy shoulder to try to hear if I could detect his voice resonating in those great lungs, but I could not. My ears were not hearing the distant song, but rather it was my heart. Its clarity and texture was similar to the sound of a train, late at night, miles away, gently sounding its horn to all who will listen in the dead of night.

Making sure not to disturb their grazing, I walked to each one and gave them a hug. I then headed towards the fence, the house, and the sleeping humans who had no idea that a chorus was being sung only several feet away. I climbed the fence, and as I spun around to flip over to the other side, I noted that Bart's head was ten feet up in the air. His ears were up and alert, and his eyes stared right straight at me. I froze, smiled, and whispered aloud, "We are almost there, my friend; we are almost there. Our promise to you we will keep; the killing is about to end." Bart nodded, and Ethan snorted. I dropped to the ground and went off to bed: to dream, to hope, and to hum. It was such a beautiful song.

CITIZEN COMPLAINT

He had never done anything like this before, he thought, as he twisted in the folding chair. The fluorescent lights of the city council meeting room made the sweat on his forehead shine like a dusting of diamonds on a black sand beach. He twisted and rolled the papers that he held in his hand, as he nervously glanced at the clock that was on the wall behind the council members. It appeared to be standing still; time had frozen.

He looked around the room, which was spotted with a few folks whom he recognized, but the rest were strangers. There had been some media people outside, but they were not allowed in. "What have I started?" he whispered. It seemed like the right thing to do last week, when the TV people got in contact with him, and interviewed and supported him. Now, sitting alone in the chambers of the city council, all eyes would be on him. He was the only one who was speaking. There were names of his neighbors on the paperwork that he held, even that of the neighborhood day care center, but he was their voice, and it was up to him to make a stand. As he squirmed and fidgeted, he ran over the facts that had brought him to this point in time: why he had raised his hand to file a complaint; why the killing of horses next to his home had finally gotten to him; why he stepped into this brave new world. As he slipped into thought, the tension dropped a peg or two.

He couldn't tell them of the noise, of the terror, of the cries of the horses as they were brought in over the weekend to be slaughtered in the pre-dawn hours of Monday morning. He couldn't tell them that, for they would not understand. He had lived next to that plant for years and tried to block it out of his mind. He had been somewhat successful, until he started to listen and hear. Those cries from the horses were once a backdrop for country living, the whinnies in the distance. It all alluded to some sort of country charm, or so he thought. Then he began to hear emotion in those calls. There were screams of loneliness, fear, and confusion. Sometimes, when he would lie in the hammock in his back yard and doze off into a Sunday afternoon nap, he would hear voices. The distant sounds of the horses came to be a dreaded addition to his life.

Then, early one Monday morning, he had his windows open, as the temperature was just right. The sounds of the crickets and tree frogs were a natural lullaby. All was good and quiet, until the killing started. He had never heard it before. Perhaps there was something wrong with the plant's air conditioning and their windows were open, or maybe it was that the wind was just right that day. Those could be some of many circumstances that forced him to hear the death screams and strangled sufferings. Hundreds of gentle and trusting horses were herded cruelly into chutes where they were locked in with bolt guns charging for their foreheads. They were then hung by a leg, and slit at the throat. Many coughed and strangled on their own blood, as they were still alive and left hanging to bleed out. He could hear them. He lay in a pool of sweat in his bed with tears in his eyes and fire in his stomach. Before he could regain control of his senses, he vomited.

They would not understand all of that, as it spoke to the heart. It was charged with emotion, and his complaint had to be grounded in facts. He was left with the issue of the smell and stench that wafted over the walls of the slaughterhouse. It was the stink of death and rotting entrails that was the basis of his complaint. It hurt him to the core to resort to something so common, so basic. When he yearned to speak of the facts and the real issues, he knew they would neither understand, nor care.

"It's your turn, sir."

He snapped back into reality, covered in sweat from the trip back in time. He fumbled with his papers and almost knocked over the folding chair as he stood up in a start.

"It's your turn," the kind lady repeated from behind the bench. The mayor smiled at him, and with that singular act of kindness, he began to feel the tension bleed away.

As he walked slowly up to the podium with his head bowed, he thought he heard whispers. It seemed that the room was full and there were whispers being passed amongst the crowd. He reached the podium, set his paperwork down, and took one look backward around the room only to find that it was nearly empty; yet, it was alive with whispers of encouragement and support. He allowed himself a second to permit the Force to wash over him and both cleanse and refresh his soul. He took a deep breath, looked at the mayor, and spoke confidently. As he spoke, he felt a cool assurance creep over him, and an upwelling of confidence filled his soul. He smiled and he gestured, and he made his point. From somewhere, far away, he thought he heard a distant horse whinny—one of joy, one of peace. The echo of that cry of hope bounced through his head as he made his stand for the horses, to stop the killing.

LOVEFEST

I slowly pushed open the backdoor. It was early morning. The sun had already risen above the tree line to the east and the bright, white German Shepherd that guards the back entrance was ready to play. He bounced several times and came to rest pressed against my lower legs, waiting to be scratched. As I gave him his morning rubdown, I again pondered on how over 100 pounds of pure muscle could bounce that high. I thought that maybe I should experiment and see how high I could bounce. Quickly, I reminded myself of the time of day, age, effort, etc., as reality gently settled back over the early morning scene. I could vault the fence, though...that was true.

Off to the west, I could see that all of the horses were leisurely grazing in the pasture so I challenged Kenny, the German Shepherd, to a race across the backyard. I then artfully vaulted the pasture's fence as skillfully as if I were still a twenty-year old. I turned and looked back at Kenny who was standing some ways off due to the "Invisible Fence." He was wagging his tail and smiling, which inherently makes him look like the Coca-Cola polar bear. "I'll be back," I called. I then turned my attention to the horses, none of which had even stopped grazing to look up at me.

It had been a week since I had been with them, not by design—but I don't know how to describe it. Perhaps it was fear that kept me away or maybe it was even embarrassment for my species. I had covertly visited one of the three horse slaughterhouses in the United States and had heard and seen more than most need to experience in a lifetime. It had changed me. A week later, others who had gone through that change had implored me to get back with the horses. They would not see what I saw, nor hold it against me, as they knew anyway. Heck, Ethan told me about it over a year ago. Why stay away? Now, here I was, in their environment, ready to heal. Quietly, I walked over to one of the oak trees and sat down to watch the horses. I did not want to press, pressure, or change them in any way; I would just sit and watch.

After several minutes, Ethan looked up, as he was the closest, perhaps 100 feet away. He turned his head towards me, smiled, and went back to eating. *Hmmmm,* I thought, *I don't rate much in the attention department.* Suddenly, it occurred to me that I was a trusted member of the herd; I walked amongst them, as would another horse and that acknowledging me might be more insult than compliment. I smiled and waited.

Finally, the one furthest away with his back to me, little Pele, turned and became immediately alarmed when he saw me sitting on the ground against the tree. Head held high, he began to prance in alarm back and forth, until I said, "It's me, Pele." In a glorified trot, he came straight towards me.

"Well…what…I never…had no idea—what are you doing on the ground? You look so small; you startled me," he panted as he approached.

Evidently, his rapid advance towards me alarmed Harley, who spun around and partially intercepted the little guy. "Slow it down, kid. You are bigger than you think, and you could hurt someone running towards them at that speed."

Pele dropped down to a walk, and Harley decided that it would be best to accompany him over to my position.

"What are you doing, Dad?" asked Pele as he sniffed and then mouthed my bare feet. "Wanna play? Let's play, Dad!" he continued, as I pushed his head away.

Harley leaned over me and nipped at Pele's cheek. "Be careful, he is smaller than us and not a minor player in the herd. Show some respect." Harley stood over me but, as usual, Pele continued to press the issue. I decided to stand up, as there were eight hooves only inches from where I sat.

"Morning, guys," I said as I hauled my aging carcass to an erect position. "I have missed you all."

Pele grabbed the tail of my T-shirt and tugged. "Let's play," he mumbled.

This time Harley nipped him and Pele stepped back several feet. "Enough," grunted Harley. Pele groaned and walked behind the tree to sulk.

Harley turned back to me, and I stroked his forehead. I decided just to listen, as I did not know what to say. It was important to absorb their feelings and not to dwell on the events of the past week.

I grabbed the knot of mane between Harley's ears and rubbed. "That feels good," he said. "Thanks!" Then he picked his head up and stared straight at me.

"I don't speak with you much as that has been Ethan's job; but, today, I want to say thank you," he sighed.

"Thank you? Thank you for what?" I asked.

"Just listen. Don't cloud the issue, as there are too many 'thank yous' to list. I do not have that much time, but thank you and your human friends for what you are doing. That is why you are here, and that is what we have been training you to do for years. It has not been an easy task; you are not an easy student to teach, but you are beginning to do what it is you need to do and we all thank you for that," he said.

"Yes, thank you," came another voice over my shoulder. It was Bart. He had joined us and hung his head over my right shoulder.

"You have never talked to me before, Bart," I whispered.

"I know, nor have the others. That was Ethan's job, but now you are ready, and we are so glad that you have listened," he said, as I reached for his forehead.

"Can we play yet?" asked Pele from behind the tree.

"*No!*" snorted the two Thoroughbreds who, when they turned to holler, made me duck as their heads swung around. Pele, a typical little colt, stomped the ground with a rear hoof and sighed.

"It's not over, but you are getting closer," said a third voice, as Ethan joined the crowd.

"You did a pretty good job with him," said Harley, "even though you are just an Appaloosa."

"Yup, good job," Bart added as he then turned to scratch and nibble on Ethan's withers. Harley stepped backwards and began to scratch on Ethan's backside. Ethan smiled and snorted, "I agree; good job."

I reached for Ethan's forehead and whispered, "I don't want you to know what I know."

Ethan pulled his head away, "Silly student, do you not remember one of our first conversations? We already know. We feel it all; everything is interconnected and the pain runs through all that are alive. 'Do not want you to know.' Have you forgotten your ties, your roots, and your heritage? Do not consider yourself to be special for seeing and hearing all that is evil and for witnessing the death of our brothers. We hear it all."

"I'm sorry," I said. I stepped back as the Thoroughbreds continued to groom Ethan. Somehow, he appeared more regal than I had ever seen him before. He surely was filled with the spirit of leadership as he continued. "You have not been damaged with this knowledge, but instead you have been blessed as you have the physical and tangible proof to give you the strength to move forward. You and your friends have grown. You are now out of the norm, and you have been blessed with power to move forward with passion and strength," he added.

"This conversation sure changed quickly," I interjected. "One minute you are thanking me and the next you begin to preach as if I am some sort of yearling with no experience."

"Can't we just run around the pasture and nip at each other for a while?" asked Pele from behind the tree.

"No," was the response from all three. Then, from across the pasture, Apache, the quiet Brasileiro, raised his head and snorted, "Grow up!" and went back to eating. I was not sure if he was speaking to me or Pele, but it affected both of us, as Pele hung his head and nipped at the tree in frustration while I leaned against it and sighed.

The "love fest" on Ethan continued, and again he spoke to me. "We thank you for your efforts and we thank your friends. That is all a given, but you are not finished. As I have been telling you, you need to tell them, all of them, every one of them, everywhere they are. Tell them! That is your reason for living; that is why we are here. You must tell them so that it will stop."

Harley and Bart stopped their grooming and turned towards me

"Tell them so that we can rest, so that the cycle is complete," continued Ethan. "Just tell them!" The two Thoroughbreds nodded as I reached for Ethan's nose and began to rub. Harley turned and came to nudge my back; Bart twisted around and pushed his nose into my hair; Ethan buried his nose in my chest; and from around the tree, Pele grabbed the back of my shorts with his teeth and said, "I still wanna play."

Several moments passed as we stood and held each other in the pasture. It was a knot of pure love unbeknownst to the human world that swirled unsuspectingly around us.

"Tell them!"

SPECIAL MOMENTS

We are a busy lot. Balancing careers, families, activities, and saving horses can get a bit overwhelming at times. Somehow, we manage to do it with highs and lows moving through our lives like the gentle groundswell felt while out to sea: up and down, up and down. Every now and then, while on the crest of the swell, we can see that land we dream of far, far away: silver-white beaches and lush green mountains. We can see it. Those are special moments, times when the powers of the universe come in line to give us a glimpse of peace and happiness.

We all have those moments; it is not a matter of hunting them down and attempting to capture them, but a matter of recognizing them when they are upon us and allowing the magic to re-energize us. We all experience them. They might be simple, in fact so simple that they can come and go without us knowing that we have missed them. So, I watch; I listen, and yesterday, I was blessed.

It is that time of year where I need to administer a second application of Roundup along our fence lines. Roundup is the world's best weed-eater and keeps the fences looking neat and trimmed. So, in the heat of the day, I loaded a mixture of five gallons into my tank sprayer, strapped it to my back, and headed down the first thousand feet of fence. As luck would have it, Pele and Bart were napping under the shade of one of the large majestic oak trees.

The curiosity was just too much for little Pele to bear, so out he came. Normally, I would have stopped and petted him, but I was on a roll and had a lot of distance to cover. I kept walking and spraying at a pretty fast clip. Pele, only a few steps behind me on the other side of the fence, matched my pace and followed. I was not sure if it was the sound of the sprayer or the unusual contraption on my back that intrigued him. Either way, we kept walking; we were now side-by-side. He managed to reach over and snatch the straw hat from my head. As I stopped, so did he. He immediately cocked his left rear hoof and appeared quite pleased with himself. I gently removed my hat from his mouth and rubbed his forehead. I then returned to my chore and the little rascal continued to tag along. I figured that he would lose interest, but to my surprise, he did not. Onward we went until I rounded the corner and went down the front. I stopped; he stopped; I petted him and, again, he went into relax mode. It was necessary for me to do a little backtracking to continue the other direction so I began to walk back from where we came. Pele followed. I picked up speed, so did he. I began to run and he did too. Then, I started to laugh and I heard him giggle. What a sight, I am sure. When we reached the other corner of the pasture, I stopped and we communicated. It was fun.

We had connected, and he was smiling. We had shared one of those special moments, and I knew it. Life was good.

Last night, as the sun set and the temperature dropped, I climbed up on the John Deere to mow the pastures—the back was in dire need of my attention. With a cold beer positioned carefully in the fender-mounted beverage holder, I headed out into the back pasture and started to trim along the fence line. The grass, this year, is doing fantastic: lush green and showing all of the health required to sustain the herd that flourishes upon it.

As I moved slowly along the fence, the smell of the fresh cut grass brought back memories of summers long ago, when I was a boy, cutting with an old, manual, rotary mower, running fast so that I could get the chore done so that I might ride my bike down to the beach. Pushing that mower through the clover, barefooted, and dodging honeybees, I could see it all. It was a moment in time, a very special moment. Just when I didn't think it couldn't get any better than that, it did.

When I started, there had not been a horse anywhere around. But, the sound of mowing meant that Dad was in the pasture and that it was time to come and play the frozen grazing game. The players [the horses] graze in the center of the pasture, and as I continually mow in ever decreasing circles, they dare me to get close to them. Then, when I do and cannot proceed because there is a knot of horses in my way, they slowly turn and just step inside the circle to ensure that I will have to go through the entire routine the next time around. This goes on for the remainder of the mowing, and they will play the game even if I move on to another pasture.

Last night, as daylight was slipping away, I had a little time for the game. The first time I came upon the little herd, I stood up on the tractor and waved my hat over my head. Five heads went up in the air and twenty hooves began to trot around the tractor as if indignation was the order of the day. Around and around they went until I decided to join in. I jumped the tractor up into high gear and followed them around in the circle. This was fun! They picked up the pace and the circle widened; I bumped the throttle up a few more RPMs, and around the pasture we went. It suddenly occurred to me that I could not catch up with them, so I fell off and headed back towards the area that we had started. As I turned to look behind me, a herd of five horses was right on my tail, chasing me! I opened up the throttle and took off as fast as I could. They, too, poured on the power and from one pasture to another; they chased me while we all laughed. Around and around we went, into the night, making circles and loops in the grass that will take days to grow out as I failed to disengage the PTO. As we ran, I kept mowing. It was a sight to see: man, machine, and horses running off into the darkness with laughter in the air. It was truly a special moment.

When the day ended, and Terry and I were securing the house for the night, I heard a little grumbling voice outside the back door. Looking through the glass, I saw our newly adopted little German Shepherd daughter, Suzi, wagging her tail and talking. I stepped out and sat down in the breezeway to hear what she had to say. She was grateful for the attention and told me, out loud, how much fun it was to have me home playing with her throughout the day. She likes that. She really enjoyed the ride in the big red truck to go up to the gas station for tractor fuel. She told me while I stroked her 'frinkled' brow that she really liked it here and did not want to leave. I interrupted her to let her know that she was welcome in our home and that she would be going nowhere. Afterwards, I whispered, "I love you!" In the darkness, I could feel her soft eyes on my face. I bent down to kiss her nose. She licked my chin and lay down upon my feet. As I savored the togetherness and gently scratched her head, I could hear an owl in the distance. A gentle breeze stirred the wind chimes. I looked up at the moon over the pasture and realized: *This is a special moment*. Suzi sighed and both our souls were at peace.

Thank God for the special moments.

I BELIEVE THAT I SAW HER THIS MORNING

I believe that I saw her this morning, just a fleeting glimpse, but I feel that she was there. I knew that she had been swimming in my dreams last night. A man knows these things. Even if the birth of a new day washes away the details, the warmth and the desire, the guilt lingers on long after you have arisen from the bed. Last night we loved long, hard, and with great passion. I knew it; I could feel it; and my masculinity told me that it was so.

She first came to me when I was in my early twenties: sleek and beautiful, her nude body rippling with muscles. It was truly love at first sight, for me. She was terrified, as she had been kidnapped from her home and family; the world as she had known it was gone. The will to live had bled out of her heart and soul. She would die if I did not hold her, reassure her, and keep her breathing. For forty-eight hours, I stayed with her and held her smooth body against me while I kept her afloat and walked her around the pool. I insisted that she breathe, that she take in the life-giving air. For two days, I would not allow her soul to escape this world, for her spirit to leave as she had wanted. Two days that almost killed me: no sleep, little food, some water, and much reassurance, I, too, almost died. But we talked. First, it was her speaking of her fears, of all that was lost, of the terror of capture, and the pain of isolation. Then it was I speaking. I told her that not all humans were evil; I told her of her mission to teach and to save; I told her of my dreams to help and to make a difference. Somewhere in that exhausted mix, I told her that I loved her. We became soul mates.

We learned to play, Maleeva and me. At first, I was afraid. When her heart finally healed and when I was in the water with her, she showed her passion for life with the teeth in her mouth. My legs were striped with teeth marks; she loved me and she showed it. Every Wednesday afternoon, Saturdays, and Sundays, I would leave my human wife to dance with my newfound lover. The laughter, the joy—no one understood. The playfulness will never escape my heart. She would receive such joy from pulling down my swim trunks each time I left her pool; no human female could compare. She laughed, but only with me. We were so deeply in love. I longed to be a member of her family, Delphinsdae. I yearned to be a male of her species, Stenella Longirestris. However, I was only a man, a human man, who walked on two legs and could never be an adequate lover. I live with that guilt and inadequacy, even today.

Then I had to leave; I had to abandon my island paradise. My human mate was suffering from "Island Fever" and I was told that I needed to leave the islands that I loved, to return to the mainland where I would ultimately be betrayed. It was a human thing; I had to go. Being a human male, I did what I was told. I said my goodbyes through tear-blurred eyes. I heard the screams of pain in my numbed ears, but I did what I was told I must do. I left her.

Several weeks after I returned to the mainland, enrolled in college, and gotten a job scraping barnacles from the bottoms of boats, the letter came. It was from my Hawaiian "want to be" lover, who worked in the park with Maleeva and me. She knew the love that Maleeva and I shared. She had been both mystified and jealous, and had always wanted a piece of our love for herself. I, however, had eyes for only one. She had written to me, probably with great delight and satisfaction. She informed me of Maleeva's refusal to take nourishment after my departure and that she almost died of starvation. She told me that the pain of me leaving drove her to swim into the wall of her pool. Her suicide attempt succeeded: her nose was crushed and her skull was shattered. The marine biologists had never seen anything like that. She closed by saying that she was sorry we had never made love. For that, I did not care; but for Maleeva, my tears flowed for decades.

I believe that I saw her this morning, just a fleeting glimpse, but I feel that she was there. I know that I dreamed of her; a man knows these things. I sat on the side of the bed and told my masculinity to subside; it hurt too much. It is true; we made love in my dreams. We embraced each other at the depth of 75 feet, traveling at 25 miles per hour. It was a rush. My heart was still racing and I was breathless, but she continued to coach me. My dream-lover continued to guide me on my life quest. She whispered softly in my ear, her voice causing the hair on the back of my arms to stand up, even during daylight hours. The voice was sweet, it was pure, and it excited me to remember it in the light of day. She speaks and says that our time will come; her family's time will come. It is the horses' turn now, but then it will be theirs. She awaits me; she will love me for all eternity; and we shall once again share one another. First, I must help the horses and then I can come to her.

I believe that I saw her this morning, just a fleeting glimpse, but I feel that she was there. The mist was held low to the pastures. I could only see the backs of the horses as they grazed in the cool dense mist. It swirled around them as if it was water. Then, a dorsal fin broke the surface, but only for a second. I saw it and, way off in the distance, I heard a dolphin laugh.

I believe that I saw her this morning.

THE WINDS OF
DESTRUCTION

The horses have been turned loose in the pasture, the hanging plants have been secured, the wind chimes are down, and all equipment has been securely stowed. Now, all that is left to do is wait, wait for the storm to do what it will do.

Churning viciously out in the Gulf of Mexico is a monster called Katrina. She is the size of three states—a furious beast that breathes rain, hail, and destruction at the rate of over 165 miles per hour. It's the stuff of which science fiction movies are made. We wait, for what, we do not know.

We could have left; we had time. In fact, I tried to persuade my bride to depart with her cat yesterday morning, but she would not leave me and the rest of our family. She seems to feel that she needs to be with us. I, however, feel otherwise. We recently bought a four-horse slant load trailer just for this purpose. Now that we have five horses sharing our lives with us, we opted to stay and await our destiny.

This is not new to me. A Florida resident for several decades, I have been through my fair share of hurricanes. In fact, we are in better shape now as Laughing Horse Farm is hooked up to a new, state-of-the-art generator that will keep us in power long after those who have lost theirs are sweltering in the heat. All is well and good; that is, if anything is still left standing.

Why are we here? What is running through the minds of the horses? They know that something is wrong; they smell it; they feel it. Why are we here? Why do we live with the thought of total destruction of all material goods and the potential loss of life in the back of our minds? What made us stay?

The outer rain bands of the storm are swirling violently over our heads and the winds are picking up. As the sun sets, it casts an eerie pall over the landscape. Fractured light bounces off the massive thunderstorms. There is a feeling of impending doom in the air; you could cut it with a knife. The horses are running anxiously in the pasture while the cows are crying out from behind. They know. Why are we here? What will come? We have lost control, and have to submit. We pray for those souls that may soon depart. We are only mortal and cannot change what is certain destiny. We are diminished by the size and the immensity of what looms over our heads. We are humbled by the realization that we are not supreme in any way, shape, or form. We only do what we can. Why are we here?

RESCUE COMES FULL CIRCLE

They were in a barn with many other horses so they were not concerned when the humans first left them; they did so every night. Tonight was different, though. There was something in the air: a scent of threat, impending doom, danger, and confusion settled upon every soul in the barn.

It did not take long for the rain and the wind to come. This too was not unusual, but this night it did not quit. In fact, it did not stop; it grew ever louder and stronger for hours and hours like the roar of a giant animal. All of the horses feared for their lives. Some reared and kicked at their stall doors, others nervously circled in their enclosures, while some just stood still with their heads lowered and shivered with fear. They knew they were going to die. It was certain that the raging beast outside of their barn would get in and devour them all, as it was pushing so hard on the structure that the barn creaked and groaned as if it had developed feelings of its own. Then it was gone. The terror left and the horses thought that they might be safe.

Dawn came dark and dank. No humans came to give them water or food; there was no one there to let them out, so they stood and waited. That is what horses do, as they can do no more. They just waited, until the waters came. First, it was just a trickle running down the center aisle and then the trickle began to grow and spread. Soon, everything was covered and it began to rise. The horses thrashed at the water in their stalls. They splashed and tried to get away as it was cold, smelly, and had a bitter taste. They could not escape, and the water continued to rise. Slowly, but surely, it rose until it lapped upon their bellies. Again, they knew that death was near and, again, they waited. How long? Who knows? Horses cannot tell time, but in human terms, it was days—so the horses just waited.

Then the humans returned, they broke down the main door, popped the locks on the stalls, and led them to clean dry trailers, into which all of the horses were glad to enter. The humans spoke softly and kindly and offered each horse a handful of feed and a clean sip of water. Then they were off, whisked down the road.

These new humans brought them to a place where there were many other horses. The stalls were dry, there was feed and hay, and the water did not taste like salt. They were confused, but they were happy to be cared for, clean, and dry. No sooner did they get comfortable, when another team of humans came and loaded them back up in a trailer and took them on another long journey.

When the trailer stopped, one of the humans came in and asked the horses one-by-one if they would like to get out and meet the people who had missed them and loved them so much. There was a hush.

"Is it safe?" asked the youngest one. The human smiled. The little colt poked his head out of the door, and there was his human friend. It was a joyful meeting for all. So much so, that one horse actually jumped and ran out of the trailer to be reunited.

The human companions had lost everything: their homes, their jobs, and their entire way of life. They thought that they had lost their equine children, too, but many had not. Life had renewed meaning and hope, and as a special treat for the horses, their stable days were over, for a while. They were put out into a brightly lit green pasture to enjoy themselves. Weeks of terror and misery were behind them. They could now renew their spirits. It did not take long for them to enjoy it.

Rescue has come full circle. Life and balance are restored, once again. The storm, Katrina, is nothing more than a dimming memory.

I THOUGHT IT WAS THE
RIGHT THING TO DO

I thought it was the right thing to do. Regardless of all the groundwork, the training, and the bonding, he would try to kill me, year after year, when I attempted to ride him under saddle. After many broken bones, I thought it was the right thing to do.

I thought it was the right thing to do: to send him for professional training, natural horsemanship accomplished by a professional in our local area; to send him to school; to pull him from the herd and set things straight.

I thought it was the right thing to do: to outline a plan with the trainer should a hurricane hit, especially since his barn sat on the Vermillion River, close to the Gulf.

I thought it was the right thing to do: to be concerned about the horses suffering from Katrina, and ignore him and not support his training.

I thought it was the right thing to do: to spend not only all of my time off, but additional vacation time to rescue other horses while he wondered if I still lived.

I thought it was the right thing to do: to drive straight from the Katrina effort, in Louisiana, to our HfH ranch, in

Hitchcock, Texas to evacuate our rescue horses to Austin in preparation for Rita, and ignore him.

I thought it was the right thing to do: to assume that while moving other horses, he would be taken care of.

I thought it was the right thing to do: to not second-guess a professional.

I thought it was the right thing to do: to run a police barricade to find out what happened to him after I received a report that he was seen on CNN in neck deep water.

I thought it was the right thing to do: to mount a 4-wheeler and fight snakes while carrying firearms to locate him in a rice paddy.

I thought it was the right thing to do: to bring him home and nurse his injuries under a vet's direction.

I thought it was the right thing to do: to inform the vet, after a week of treatment, that he was not improving.

I thought it was the right thing to do: to put him, alone, in an equine hospital stall.

I was told that it was the right thing to do: to sign the release that he may pass away under general anesthesia tomorrow.

I thought it was the right thing to do for him, overall. Tonight, he is alone; I am alone; and I now question my ability to ascertain what the right thing to do is.

Tomorrow, I will await the call that he is recovering from surgery. I will be waiting for the reassurance that it was the right thing to do. Tonight, the world is an uncertain and very lonely place, as I no longer know the right thing to do.

I can only hope that he thinks and believes that I have done the right thing.

He is missed. He is the center of my thoughts and he is in my prayers. That, at least, is something to hold on to, as I know in my heart of hearts that it is the right thing to do.

I FLEW OVER KAUFMAN

I flew over Kaufman, Texas, yesterday. A common occurrence as I make this trip often. Coming from either Lafayette or Baton Rouge, Kaufman needs to be passed over to reach Dallas. I always know that it is there, but normally I never look down. Instead, I simply sit back and wrap my tattered blanket of self-actualization around myself and zone out. It's too much to process. There is too much pain and I usually just go numb. It's much easier that way, you know, it hurts so much less. Like horses, humans seek that path of least resistance and always head for their comfort zone of choice.

Yesterday it was different. I looked out the window of the plane as we took off from the DFW airport. The city slipped away beneath and behind us as we headed east. I traced out the path of I-20 and, as the plane finally eased off to starboard, there it was, 35,000 feet below, the city of death. As my eyes recognized the roads and highways, I could make out the slaughterhouse, the source of so much needless suffering. It was all laid out below me.

It was Tuesday morning and, as I gazed down on that evil place, I knew that innocent horses were being killed as I watched. As we flew by, tens of thousands of feet over their heads, souls were being wrenched from unwilling bodies. Lives that wanted to continue were being ended in a most despicable manner. I put my hand on the window and could blot out the city. Better yet, I put my finger on the window and made the plant disappear. I smiled, how easy. If only it could be so. The tension in my chest was noticeable. I began to concentrate on the souls that were departing this mean place as I watched. Did they fly screaming to the other side in abject terror? Did they rise in peace above all of this violence? Could they look down upon all of this sadness as I was now doing? If the spirits rose to the heavens on high, could I see them or feel them as I, too, flew amongst the clouds?

I held my right hand to the window, closed my eyes, laid my head back on the headrest, and allowed the drone of the jet turbines to turn into the universal mantra of meditation, "ooommmmmm." As I attempted to shut down my mind, I felt a warm tear seep out of the corner of my right eye and recklessly roll down the side of my face until it became lost in my mustache. Its final destination was lost to me, as I just felt the soft breath of an exhale in my left ear and heard a distant nicker register in my brain. My heart jumped and my breathing stopped as my nostrils filled with the sweet smell of hay at 35,000 feet. With eyes still closed and breath withheld, I reached out with my left hand just as a gentle swat of tail hair caressed my left cheek. My hand settled on muscular withers as I stroked and I scratched. The warmth and energy flowed up my arm as if I had touched an open electrical circuit. There was peace; there was anger; there was confusion; and with the intensity of emotion, there was a tremendous strength. I could feel myself being pulled into the vortex, so I attempted to clutch onto the withers to maintain my balance—only to find my hand come up empty.

My eyes popped open; my left hand was clutching the fabric of the vacant seat beside me; and I was soaked in sweat. The jet turbines droned on.

There lived, in my heart, the need to get home; the need to see and hold my equine charges; the need to continue to work on cessation of the senseless slaughter; and the need to survive and avoid being beaten down. We must win.

I looked out the window; Kaufman was long gone. A quick survey of the cabin revealed that there was no evidence of my visitor. I brushed the sweat from my brow, leaned my head back, and attempted to stop shaking. It had to stop. As a myriad of thoughts ran through my head, I was aware that there was still a presence lingering, a gift left behind from my vision, a reinforcement of what had taken place. As we dropped from the sky to make our final approach for landing, I breathed in the familiar and sweet smell of hay; it lived on. I have taken it with me as a gift, as reinforcement—the sweet smell of life.

Yesterday, I flew over Kaufman, Texas.

IT HAD BEEN A WHILE

It had been a while since they had spoken with him. They knew that he had been busy, particularly since the hurricanes. Before the storms, he used to come out and sit with them, often sharing conversation and stories over the round bale; but it had been a while. They missed the contact, but could feel the clutter in his mind and the battle raging in his soul. So, they calmly waited, knowing that he would return to them. Tonight, he was sitting on the fence, thoughtfully watching them munch on the new round bale in the back pasture.

There was a gentle thump. They all looked up to see that he had hopped off the fence and was heading their way. His features were obscured, due to the backlight effect from the barn's warm glow. They knew, however, that a smile was hidden in the approaching silhouette and they all sighed in unison as he drew near.

They taught him well on the art of listening. It had taken a few years, but one night, many weeks ago, he had heard and learned to listen. Tonight would not be one of those nights, as they could feel his spirit about to explode with the need to unload. That would be okay. They had not heard from him in so long that they would listen. There was not much that they could learn. But, they would listen to his tales of human misery and be thankful that he carried those tales to them to share.

They closed their eyes and continued to eat, welcoming him to join them.

He walked amongst them, lightly stroking each one and uttering soft verbal welcomes. Gently, he moved up to the round bale and began to pick leaves and sticks out of it so that it would be easier to eat. They liked this. They always liked him to eat with them at night as it made them feel safe. They all closed their eyes and listened as his mind tried to organize its thoughts. It was a mess, and he apparently knew it.

As he passed his hands over the round bale, he tried to apologize. He attempted to say that he was sorry for being so distant and, true to human form, he attempted to rationalize and make excuses. What he did not know was that they needed no apologies or excuses; they were simply glad that he was there in the "here and now." They let him go on uninterrupted, as it appeared to be helping him.

He told them stories of human injustices, and he showed them images that made them glad that they were not human. He cried a few tears of frustration and then spoke to them of love. He was sincerely full of love on many levels, and this drove him mad. His heart went out to them, their brothers, their cousins, and all who could not speak for themselves. He yearned to express his caring to his mate, his family, his friends, and to all of his four-legged children. Over half a century old, he was still like an infant when it came to expressing those feelings. He rattled on and on and on, until the Appaloosa gently rested his chin upon his shoulder and whispered in his ear. The others watched. The Mustang colt moved near to touch him, too; and then, he quieted while he opened up and listened to the words of truth and inner peace.

She rolled over in the bed and opened her eyes to look at the clock. It was 2:00 a.m. and it then dawned on her that there was no large, masculine shape between her and the clock. She was alone in bed.

Quietly, like a cat, she slipped from under the covers, donned her robe and slippers to check the spare bedrooms to see if he may have gone to bed in another room so as not to wake her. All beds were neatly made and empty. She proceeded to the living room, then to the den where he often fell asleep in his easy chair. She then went to the laundry room where she had an unobstructed view of the guest house or the "Man Cave" as he so liked to call it. He would frequently sneak out there to write or curl up on the couch and watch television, in secret; but all lights were off. She then sighed, kicked off her slippers, and pulled on her muck boots to head outside. It was a bit nippy.

As she exited the back door and made her way around the garages, she could see that all of the lights were on in the barn. "Aha," she whispered, "so that is where he is." She did not call out, as she did not want to wake the German Shepherds, who were safely asleep in their dog house. She scurried to the barn only to discover that it, too, was empty. She walked to the back barn door to peer out into the dark pasture and could see nothing but several figures standing near the round bale, under the light, behind the "Man Cave." From the barn, she could not make out the congregation so she exited the barn to walk the fence line to the round bale.

The grass was wet, but the boots kept her feet dry. For some reason, a portion of her soul wanted to feel anxious as to her husband's absence. Another part of her, however, was whispering that it was alright. As she neared the bale, she could see the Brazilian Mangalarga off in the dark. He was several dozen yards away sleeping, yet pointed towards the others at the bale. That was typical, as he was a tad standoffish but, again, he was the big protector.

Her pulse quickened. She uttered a small gasp when she came abreast of the bale and saw him lying on the ground with his back planted upright and his legs splayed out in the hay. She then quietly inhaled when she noted that the little Mustang colt was laying next him with his head in her husband's lap. On the other side was the Appaloosa, sitting like a reproduction of the Sphinx with his front legs tucked under his body, looking dreary-eyed at her. Standing on either side, above them, were the Thoroughbreds, both with back feet cocked and heads dipped low in gentle sleep.

She froze for a moment as she knew the danger that he was in should she spook one causing them to unwittingly step on him. She then took in the expression on his face: eyes closed, and mouth frozen in a gentle smile. Her heart melted as she looked at the horses that both stood and lay around him. She actually felt as if she were an intruder into a very special and intimate moment. The Appy yawned and smiled at her; she smiled back and turned towards the house. As she walked back, a warm glow washed over her and buoyed her towards her bed. As she slipped between the covers, it never occurred to her to check to see if he had been breathing. The thought had not been an issue.

To this day, she does not know when he slipped back between the covers and held her in his arms; her sleep was not disturbed, her dreams were sweet, and he was, oh, so very warm. As they lay with their souls intertwined, the horses ran through their dreams: there was the pounding of hooves, a distant whinny heard under a glorious sunrise, and the sweet smell of hay. Their spirits were one and, for that singular fleeting moment, they were at peace. It had been a while.

I HEARD HIM, BUT DID NOT LISTEN

He was the first one, my first friend upon returning to the United States, that is. I had a previous friend that I was forced to leave behind, many miles away and south of the equator. The pain of that parting still lingers in my heart and I was certain that the void would never be filled. I will forever treasure the memories of playing on the beach and running through the mountain rainforest, but I never moved on.

He was the first one, the first one that we bought to save from going to slaughter, the first American horse to grace our barn. Terry took to him instantly; they appeared to be soul mates. Then, the drugs from the horse trader wore off and we realized that we had "saved" something that breathed fire and considered humans to be good for one thing—killing. He raged, attacked, broke through fencing, and kicked me to the ground. I told Terry that he needed to go. He was hopeless. He would kill one of us, but she stood her ground and said "no." So, the years slipped by.

As time passed, he calmed. He watched and observed us and, every day, he received a small dose of love. He observed us interact with each other, the other horses, and the dogs. He saw love.

Then one day, he spoke to me. He told me that he was sorry for the loss of life that happened over our heads. He let me know that they knew that the spacecraft had fallen and heard the spirits move on. He conveyed this to me several years ago, which I wrote down, and then moved on.

He continued to speak to me as the years passed; he told me that he was teaching me. He explained who and what horses are and he pushed me to help others and learn to listen. I heard him and thought I understood. Again, I moved on.

He has been out in the pasture for years, only seeing me on rare occasions. I considered him to be nothing more than an ornament on our property. He was written off...loved, but not involved, and not paid much attention. Yet, he continued to talk. He spoke to me often in my dreams, his hooves pounding, his distant whinny; I would hear him almost daily. I was not aware that he was speaking to someone else, asking for her help. He insisted that she get me to listen, to understand, to comprehend, and to let go.

She listened; I did not. She understood where I could care less. Then, one day, she took my hand and re-introduced me to him, helped me ask permission to partner with him and assisted me on his back. I had no fear, no trepidation, and no expectations, just a quiet satisfaction that we had found each other.

With that confidence, for the first time as partners, he and I left the confines of what had been his home for many years. We walked as one up the driveway and through the gate to experience the world with Terry, riding her soul mate, Apache, at our side. We left our bounds behind and allowed the sun to dance on us as the cool wind whipped through our hair. We walked and trotted, and saw scenes of the world that we had never seen before. We laughed and loved from afar, as our partners bore us upon their backs and shared in our joy. It had been many years since I had felt this way, partnered with family and friends. My spirit was set free while tied to a giant companion who understood every movement of my body and reacted to the gentlest of touches. It was heaven on earth.

While we walked, he occasionally looked back at me as if to verify the expression on my face. He was not disappointed. Yet, I stroked his withers to assure him that all was well.

Upon return to our gate, I allowed him to move as he saw fit. He walked right past the property entrance, anxious to walk on and explore more. Sadly, that would not be the case. Human obligations bound me to other activities, so we headed home.

I spoke to him as I gently removed his tack. He lowered his head kindly for me to remove the bridle and bit. He stood still as I removed our saddle and pad, and he did not flinch when I gave him a cleansing shower. I spoke to him and said "Thank you" as I brushed him down. Terry came over, gave him a big hug, and whispered "Thank you" in his ear; she now had someone to ride with her. I watched the tears form in her eyes and as she hung around his neck, he turned his head to me and softly put his left nostril in my right ear, "Thank you," he sighed. "Thank you for finally listening." He pulled his head away so that the big Appaloosa eye could look directly at me. My eyes got wet and so did his. Terry let go and, in unison, the three of us said, "I love you," with no coaching or direction; it just happened. I had finally listened.

HIS EYES UPON ME

I could feel someone watching me, looking, and inquiring with curious eyes—not that I found it disturbing. Many creatures, both man and beast would look at me, some with loathing while others stared as if I were their next meal. But, this was different. There was a feeling of intense interest, a caring that seemed to smooth down my back just as surely as if someone caressed me with a physical hand. It was pleasant, and I enjoyed the ocular attention from afar.

At first, the feeling came as a fleeting moment. Then, with each passing day, it seemed to increase in both intensity and duration. Finally, I took note of the time of day and location of this pleasant event, so that I could perhaps learn the source.

At my age, the days held little excitement, so my routine was easy to follow. At night, I would sleep in the grass across from the large people-dwelling. Then, when the sun peeked above the horizon, I would wander down into the swamp where the tall grass grows, and dine at the water's edge. When the shadows would lengthen, I would return from whence I came before the night-prowling swamp crocodiles decided to make me their dinner. I always would return to stay near the big people-dwelling, as there was light. The light gives one comfort when sleeping alone in the bush. It does have its drawbacks, though. With all of the noise, commotion, and smells generated by the people, they bring one no peace. But, somewhere out there, one of them was watching me, looking for me. That attention was stirring feelings that I had not felt for many, many years.

My routine told me that I would feel this sensation in the evening, just as the sun was disappearing. It seemed as if it came from the large people-dwelling. So, after days of basking in this warm glow, I was astonished when it was not there one evening. I stood across the road from the large people-dwelling, but nothing was there. So, I hung my head, chewed on some grass, and attempted to forget about the hollow feeling that was eating at my soul.

All of a sudden, I felt the warmth; only it was more intense than ever. When I raised my head, there was a human male standing across the road, smiling and watching me with soft eyes. We looked at each other for several moments, and I could see sadness in his eyes and feel pain in his heart. This confused me. Though I did not understand, I was very pleased by his presence.

After a few moments of watching each other, he began to walk towards me steadily and with great confidence; without wavering, he closed the gap between us. Normally, I would have been prompted by my instincts to flee, as few humans have approached me for nothing other than evil purposes; but his closeness was welcomed. He had his head lowered out of respect, his eyes gently peering at me. I could see a broad smile across his face. Before I knew it, he was standing right next to me just a few feet away. As he raised his head with that warm big smile, he slowly extended his arm and put the back of his hand before my nose for inspection.

I respected this courtesy and obligingly took a few sniffs from the skin on his hand. The scent was not one that I could place, nor was it native to my habitat. It was fresh, clean, and held an essence of happiness and goodness in it, alien to my native surroundings.

Just as slowly as he had raised it, he lowered his hand and confidently stepped over to my left side and began to stroke and rub my withers. I almost fell over from the pleasure. No one or nothing had given me any sort of tactile sensation or relief for many years. My knees grew weak, and I feared that I might fall over.

Then he gently stroked me down my back, making ever-greater swirls and curls in his movements. I was trying to be strong, but I knew that I was beginning to weave where I was standing. The impulse to breathe struck me as I had been holding my breath, so I exhaled and took in a deep lungful of fresh air.

Next, he curled his hand around my side and scratched the skin on my chest right between my two front legs—you know…in that spot that you cannot reach. My eyes rolled back into their sockets, my head thrust forward, and my bottom lip stuck out while the top lip flapped up and down mouthing words that I could not even understand. What was he doing to me? Then he stopped, whispered something in me ear, and was gone in a flash.

What? What had I done? "No, don't go," I tried to call out, but he quickly disappeared across the street and through the gate and into the large people-dwelling.

My legs were still weak, my pulse was still racing, and my breathing was heavy when he reappeared. He was running out of the gate with something in his hands. He had only been gone a few moments, but it seemed like an eternity. My heart almost leapt out of my chest when I saw him coming back to me. Who was this human who had touched me so deeply and so very, very quickly? My question did not continue to hold my interest, as what he had in his hands snapped me suddenly to attention. Here, running towards me, was a human carrying a large container of food, fruit, and nourishment. Suddenly, my interest in the human disappeared as my stomach began to churn and gurgle. Each step brought the food that much closer to me.

I slowly took several steps in his direction as he approached me with a banana extended out in front of my nose.

That delicious and sweet smell was one I had not encountered in many years, so I obligingly opened my mouth and took a firm bite. It tasted even better than I remembered. He held the remainder for me so that I could chew what I had taken, and then I grabbed some more. It felt so good sliding down my throat. The sensations were almost as intense as from the contact just a few moments before. While I ate, he talked to me; at least, that was what I thought he was doing. His mouth was moving and soft, gentle sounds were coming out. The sounds felt good, almost as good as the food, but instead of filling my stomach, the sounds were food for my soul.

I tried to interpret the sounds, but they were just like the sounds of a bird singing. As we stood there and I listened, I began to pick up another voice, another picture coming to me when I closed my eyes. It was him. He was speaking to me as we speak to our own kind—through our hearts. Softly and gently, with the physical sounds acting as a backdrop, he was asking me about myself, imploring me to tell my story as he stood quietly and listened. So, with a mouth full of grapes, I began to speak to him from my heart and share with him the story of my life, as I knew it. As I allowed the feelings to play backwards and the emotions to wash over us, he remained quiet. I could feel great sadness coming from him that I did not understand. This was my life; I knew no different. Yet, the story of my years appeared to sadden him, and he softly stroked me while my soul sang its song.

The hours must have slipped by quickly for, when I opened my eyes, it was dark. He was still there, standing beside me with his arm gently wrapped around my withers, and tears streaming down his face. I tried to ask what was wrong, but he hushed me and continued to stroke me.

After a long silence, I could hear him whisper from deep within my heart. He said that he wished he could take me home with him, far away, where he and others of his kind help horses have a better life. He told me of happy places where horses are safe; where horses are loved; and where horses can have a wonderful time just being horses. It sounded like a dream to me. He spoke with such sincerity; I knew it to be true. I tried to tell him that I was fine; this was all I have ever known and as long as I was not beaten or attacked, it was a good life for an African horse.

He sighed somewhere within my heart and told me that he would be back, and while he was away, he would tell my story to others and repeat the saga that I had just relayed to him. He was sure that out there, someone would be moved by what

I had said and maybe that someone would make a difference and do the right thing. He said my story was one of hope and that he would share it. These words made me feel warm; it made the light within my soul shine a little brighter, and then he said "goodbye."

Although I wanted to beg him to stay, the power in his goodbye and the parting words that he would be back gave me strength. I sighed goodbye and watched his warmth and love ebb out of me as he walked off into the darkness. I stood there, alone, in the dark for a few minutes; I felt his eyes upon me from afar one last time; and then, my soul chilled.

I think of him often; the sun has come and gone many times since our encounter. I come and stand outside the big people-dwelling every evening and long for his gaze, but the only attention I receive is a few rocks thrown at me from wandering boys. The other day a dog thought that I might be a good snack, but he quickly learned differently.

I stood alone in the dark and stared at the dwelling, wondering what it was that I said that upset him so. It was a simple story, a story of how my life has progressed, and the struggles that I have fought. Yet, it all seemed to be too much for his soul to bear. I wondered where he came from, what he knew that I didn't know back in that land where horses are treated well. He said that people actually tend to horses and feed them regularly. This, I would like to see. He told me that people actually love horses, unlike the way people of my land treat horses. I wonder if maybe it all was a dream that my old soul pulled up, and I thought was real. Could so kindly a human really have treated me like that? Did a human really ask to hear my story? Did I, for a few moments, glimpse another world or maybe the world to come? Was my vision of my own making? Was he a human or was he a spirit from that other magical world that he spoke of with such clarity?

I stood alone in the dark before the great people-dwelling, heart a swirl with emotions from afar. What was he, who was he, was he coming back? A lizard skittered across the grass before me; a dog barked some distance away; and the continual din of human noise lay across the steamy night like fog on an open pasture.

I hung my head; my eyelids slowly slid down; and, as I tuned out what was around me, I listened to my heart speak words of wonder. Far away, as if there was an entire universe between us, I heard him whisper and sigh, "I'll be back." I called back with a nicker and then allowed sleep and happiness to wash over me. He will be back.

AUTHOR'S NOTE:

This is the story of an old and battered mare that I met on Lekki Island, outside of Lagos, Nigeria. Every evening I would stand in my hotel room and look across the jungle and open field to see her standing there, alone, in the evenings. One night, I could not resist the temptation to go and meet her. In reality, I needed a horse fix myself, as I was a world away from my family.

I was pretty shocked by what I saw: worm belly, open sores covered with flies, and hooves totally out of control. There were marks and tears on her skin that looked like she had been hacked at with machetes, which could have been the case. The very sight of her broke my heart.

For all of the evidence of past abuse, she showed me no fear, only curiosity. It almost was as if she never had been approached with compassion or interest. It was more than she could stand; in fact, she took the first step towards me.

I spent a lot of time with her that evening, and yes, she had a story to tell. What amazed me most was that there was no regret; there was no lamenting; and there was not a hint of a whine. She knew no different. This was the baseline of her life and she had experienced no good with which to compare it. And, so, as it is with many people in this part of the world, they know no different. They have always lived in squalor; hence, it is the norm. That is what she taught me that night. She was not suffering in her heart, as it was all that she knew; the thought of anything better was a concept never pondered. So, for the several weeks that I was gone from her land, I wrestled with what she had taught me and was looking forward to seeing her again.

Upon my return, she was gone. I watched every night for weeks, but she never returned. So, one humid Nigerian evening, I walked across the street into the tall grass again. I was hoping to find a clue; to catch a feeling; to sense her presence, but she was gone. The tropical breeze caused the tall reed grass to rustle and the palms to dance, yet she was nowhere to be seen. I closed my eyes, took a deep breath, and called to her from deep within me. Even internally, all was quiet; but my memories were still intact and I could see her standing before me, enjoying my touch, munching on the fruit, and sharing her story. The vision caused me to smile, to feel very much alone, and to remember my promise. "I will tell them your story," I had said, and she had asked, "Why?" "Because, maybe it will touch someone who can make a difference; all it takes is one." And, with that, she had smiled; not fully understanding, but she had smiled.

It is my hope that one day I can sit down and write that story; a story of struggles, pain, suffering, and triumph. I hope that I can do her justice and share her pride. I hope that out there, somewhere, she is smiling—smiling because she knows that she has made a difference. Halfway around the world, her tale has touched a few human hearts.

It is also my hope that she continues to smile. For the first time in her long life, she experienced the feeling of love that was given freely and returned unfettered.

I just hope that she is still smiling.

SHE HAD NO WAY OF KNOWING

She stood in a dimly lit, narrow alleyway with just four other horses ahead of her. She was the last one in line followed only by a mean-spirited human who prodded her with a stick every time a horse at the front of the line was pushed through the doors ahead. The doors simply snapped open and the crowded horse would leap forward to escape. Instantly, it slammed shut followed by, not only mechanical and unknown sounds, but by the soul rendering screams of horses in agony. She had no way of knowing where she was.

As the poking and prodding grew more intense and the screams grew ever closer, she had no way of knowing that for years, people across the nation and around the world were sweating blood and crying tears to prevent her from being pressed against those very same doors.

She had no way of knowing, as she was forced through the doors and into the confining shoot, that only a pen and a piece of paper stood between her life and her death.

When the bolt gun hit her forehead and she jerkily crumpled to the floor, her bladder emptied. She had no way of knowing that the humans around the shoot were enjoying this last kill. They resented her life and her very essence.

As the chain from the winch was wrapped around her left rear hoof and she was hoisted brutally into the air, she had no way of knowing that people would be celebrating this day as a happy, triumphant occurrence.

While the knife cleanly yet cruelly slit her throat and her own warm blood ran down her face and into her dilated nostrils, she had no way of knowing that the event of her death would be documented, cherished, and revered for all time. The senseless killing was over.

And finally, as her spirit unwillingly was jerked from her butchered and mutilated body, she had no way of knowing that she was truly, the last one—the last horse to be killed in the U.S. for human consumption in lands far, far, away. She was the last one to suffer, the last one to die, the last one to cry out, and the last one to be lost.

She had no way of knowing....

FIREWORKS

Last night, July 4, I entered Terry's office to shut down the computer before heading to bed. Everyone else was tucked away, and I was doing the last minute security sweep, when my eye's caught the bright glare of a fireworks rocket heading for the stars in the northern sky. When it reached its pre-destined point of suicide, it erupted into a brilliant display of red and blue stars cascading downward across the acres of millet that separate us from a distant subdivision. I walked closer to the window when, suddenly, the noise of the explosion reached our farm. BOOM! As the sound trailed off, another took its place— the thunder of hooves. The horses were freaked.

I ran out the back door and looked over our compound's rear fence. I could just make out, by the glow of the barn's back security light, a multi-colored, many-legged mass working up and down the back fence. The boys were *not* happy.

I called them, jumped the fence, and began to whistle the comforting dinner whistle. Although they slowed, they would not come any closer, as I was several feet nearer to the terrifying sight and noise. Continuing to walk towards the moving mass of fur, feet, and ears, I knew that there were a few bulging eyes in that mess. The darkness, however, covered the evidence.

As I neared, Apache, the tough little Brasileiro, peeled off from the herd and planted himself in the middle of the pasture staring at the source of the commotion. I let him be as he was making his statement that he was tough, cool, and the big man on the farm. Standing at only 14.3 hands, he suffers from chronic short-man syndrome. Again, I whistled, as I planted myself next to the back fence. I was particularly careful that in the dark I not touch the electrified rope that keeps the boys away from that single strand of my neighbors barbed cow wire. I only had on sandals, and touching that now would result in all five hairs on my head sticking straight up. That would surely terrify Terry when I finally made it to the bedroom.

Apache stood his ground and, in the dim light, I could both see and feel two Thoroughbreds, one Appaloosa, and a little Mustang mix headed towards me in full gallop. It was a pretty sight, but rather disconcerting as I failed to bring out any protection—not even a lead. I hollered "Whoa!" and walked towards them. They split up, and in an instant, I was surrounded by heavy breathing and horse noses tapping me on the shoulder and the back of the head. Harley steamed up my glasses as if he wanted to verify my identity.

As the horses milled about me, I listened and watched as their individual personalities materialized both to my eyes and to my ears. Ethan instantly became brave with me standing beside him. He planted himself firmly on the ground looking in the direction of the fireworks with his ears pointed forward—a virtual pillar of strength. Should I move, however, he would, too, and not allow the gap between us to be any greater than just a few feet. Of course, that was not due to fear, but rather comradeship.

Then there was Harley, slowly circling and finally standing behind Ethan and me. Although he wanted all to believe that he was the toughest and the greatest, he would gladly give over the title of Pasture King to anyone who would take it in a time of crisis.

Big nervous Bart continued to pace the fence line with the little Mustang baby carefully tucked between him and the fence. Little Pele kept peeking over Bart's back to see what I was going to do to make the fiery noisy monsters go away.

I calmly leaned over, reached to the Earth, and jerked up a handful of grass as if I was grazing. I kept this process up as I drifted further and further away from the back fence. The notion that I was calm enough to graze pulled all of the horses to me, with the exception of Apache. He was firm in his stance. As the horses calmly came around me, I heard the whispers and the soft gentle sounds of expression that I have learned to love. They come so rarely, but when they do, it is so special. I listened and did not cloud their words with my inquiries.

"What are those things?" panted little Pele. "I have never, ever, seen anything like that. Do they eat horses?"

"We don't think so," answered Harley, "but we are safe now that Gray Mane is out here."

"We were safe long before he ever showed up," countered Ethan. "The fact that he is here shows that they are a special thing, and he is only here to help us learn from them."

Bart replied, "Man, you're smart. I thought that someone was shooting at us and that we were all doomed."

Having enough of the chit-chat, Apache slowly turned his head and snorted, "You *all* are a bunch of sissies!" Then he laughed.

I laughed, too, and when I did, they all turned to look at me, then at each other, and then at me again. It was truly a "Kodak Moment." The horses looked at each other, and then looked at me. You could clearly hear them say, "Does he hear us?" The look of shock and surprise was priceless.

Ethan moved away from the others and pressed his nose against my chest. "Yes he does. I forget this as it does not happen often, but I was the one that taught him to listen."

Without giving away my secret, I stroked Ethan's forehead, looked directly into his left eye, and smiled. He put his left nostril into my right ear and exhaled, "And I hear you, too," he said.

We then turned towards the north, standing behind Apache, and watched the fireworks with Ethan to my right, Harley to my left, Bart with his head over my right shoulder, and little Pele goosing me in the left kidney. "Can I come in with you tonight, Dad? Please? Can I come in, huh, can I?" I turned and petted his head, smiled, and turned back to the display. Five horses and one human watched in awe. None of us can tell you when it was all over. The night melted away, and I do not know how or when I found my bed.

THE VALLEY OF LAUGHTER

It's rare to find one's self in another land, a different world, without even remembering how, when, or where you passed a boundary. Granted, the journey is a long one: up and down California mountain roads past many gorgeous vistas. First, the roads are paved and spread out in multiple lanes. Then, they twist and wind about until they are only two lanes, then one, next gravel, then dirt, and as you pull up to the mystical entrance gate, only one vehicle could make its way through at a time.

Perhaps it is when you step out of your earthbound vehicle, at the gate, that you know you are getting close to a place that is truly different, unique, and very special. Maybe it is the wooden fence rails that run beside you, bound together by hand with rope. Perhaps it is the vibrant hand-painted welcome sign that reads, in a brilliant blue, "Circle 7," or, perchance, it is the whispering in the leaves of the trees. Yes, perhaps that is it. From overhead and far away, the leaves in the trees whisper a distant laugh, a barely audible giggle, and a sigh of happiness. Yes, that is when you first are aware that you have arrived.

As you drive through the narrow gate and up the path, you pass a series of barns on your right. There, several free-roaming horses, many very large, look your way, smile, and nod. The whisper of laughter is heavy in the air. As you make a sharp turn to the left and descend into the valley you may pick up several companions: dogs, running beside you with mouths in an open smile while tongues bounce to and fro as they keep pace with your motorized decent. More sounds of happiness seep in through your vehicle's ventilation system. A smile breaks across your face.

When you slowly and carefully make your way down to the valley floor, you feel that perhaps you have truly passed into another time or dimension, as off to the right in the distance, two Native American teepees stand majestically in a clearing under ancient oak trees. Then, after you pass through another gate into the main yard, there is a quaint turn-of-the-century bathhouse to your right. Nestled into the mountainside, on your left, is a clean-cut two-story building that reminds you of a schoolhouse from years gone by, right down to the cupola atop the shinning metal roof. From its ample porch, your hostess, the sole human inhabitant of this valley, waves and smiles a big welcome.

You have arrived at a very special place, and within seconds, you are blessed with the sound of laughter ringing from the sides of the mountain and across the valley floor. This incredibly extraordinary residence has been carved out of the wilderness by one of America's last, true, pioneer woman. Over the years, living first in a tent, then in the teepees, and finally in the gallery/home, this woman has made this unique plot of land a place for her to work, a place for her to live, and a place for her to love and be loved by the animal companions that fill her life with joy. This is the home of equine artist, Leslie Anne Webb.

One feels privileged to walk upon this sacred ground. Many years of toil and tears went into making it the place of sharing that it is today. The original intent was to create an environment conducive for working with oils and telling the individual stories of horses through immortalizing their likenesses in paintings. The painting turned out to be the easy portion of this long and incredible journey. Along the way, horses were rescued, wells were dug, dogs were saved, and buildings were built. All accomplished through the hands of this artist and the spirit that makes this country great.

One can easily get lost in hearing the stories of challenge, triumph, and ultimate victory. In fact, before you realize it, an entire day can slip through your fingers as quickly as if you had fallen over a waterfall. Listening to Leslie, while rubbing down the horses and petting the dogs, causes a shift in the normal time continuum and you soon find yourself longing to go back to the beginning and start all over again. Sadly, even in this magical valley, the earth will not spin in reverse. Therefore, you must relent, say your goodnights, and if you are lucky enough, you head off to the teepees to refresh and recharge both body and soul.

During the night, you can still hear the gentle giggling amongst the leaves in the trees. In fact, you can see the limbs shiver and quake above your head through the opening in the teepee's peak. The trees dance with the wind to some ancient melody as your energy circulates around the teepee, around and upward, until in your dreams you too are dancing to a very far away, but persistent, tribal song. You sleep very, very well.

Upon wakening, you question your dreams of dancing with nature only to discover that you have been blessed and covered with a delicate blanket of oak leaves that was added to your man-made blanket during the night. Perhaps it was not a dream, after all.

Over a mug of coffee, more stories are shared, laughter rings anew, paintings are admired, and plans to save even more horses are made. You nurse the coffee, for when it is gone you must leave; so the sharing of life's tall tales continues. But time moves quickly in the valley. Soon the bottom of your coffee mug comes into view, and you must journey back into the world from whence you came.

You say your goodbyes to the rescued horses, you pet the dogs that have been saved, you stroke the cat whose life has been salvaged, and embrace the pioneer woman one last time before departing. In that last fleeting moment, you steal a departing glance at the art that she has created and gaze again at the land that she has transformed into art. From one heart, so much living beauty has been fashioned that you find a tear slowly creeping down your cheek as you reluctantly turn the key in the ignition.

A wave of the hand, the bark of a dog, and the crunch of tires on gravel signal that you are on a journey forward into time, back to the contemporary world where technology is king and where man has forgotten his roots. As you ascend out of the valley, emptiness begins to grow inside your heart, or perhaps it is only returning. Nevertheless, you desperately fight the urge to turn around.

Once through the gate, up high on the mountain, you exit your vehicle to close and latch it ensuring the safety of the horses. Above you, the leaves whisper a farewell. You linger for a moment and hold onto one of the hand-lashed fence rails while you take in the music of the trees. There, in the nearest rope lashing, you see something: a delicate object twisting in the gentle breeze. Carefully, you pluck it from between the lashings of the binding rope, and to your delight, you realize it is the ornate and delicate tail feather of a native hawk. And, as you twirl it before your eyes and absorb its beauty, you hear from very far away, echoing softly from the valley below, the cry of its owner wishing you well as you reluctantly depart the Valley of Laughter.

THE SILENCE

We knew she would be coming; she had told me so on the phone. We knew in advance that she would be alone, though it did not make it any easier. We all knew, yet we were still not prepared.

Silently, I had been waiting for her, sitting in the gazebo in the center of the pasture. Four horses surrounded me, and when Pele wasn't nudging my shoulder, Bart was resting his head on it. Harley sporadically cried out for his friend, as he would always do when they were separated. For the first time ever, Pele called to him, too. Something was different this time, something was not right. I was there, and each time Harley would call, I gently said that it was okay. He would turn and look at me with eyes full of questions. "What are you doing here?" was foremost on his mind, I am sure.

Usually, when Ethan was out of the pasture, I was with him: riding, sharing good times, and going places. But this afternoon he was gone, and I was there. The horses were confused. They saw his painful departure with her this morning. Why was I not with him? I could only whisper that it was okay.

Suddenly, the heads of the two German Shepherds, faithfully keeping watch on the other side of the fence, spun around and looked up the drive; their tails began to wag. The horses looked up. She must be home.

I could not see the entrance gate obscured behind the barn, but I heard a truck door slam, the mechanical whir of the gate opener, and amidst the sound of acorns popping under her feet on the concrete drive, I caught a glimpse of her walking towards us. She was alone.

Down the drive, across the backyard she came. Her straw hat was pulled over her eyes, and her head was bowed. There were things in her hands that I did not want to see. The horses stared as I tried to wave her off. I did not want to see. It was as if time was standing still and her walking was in slow motion. She did not waver as she headed across the pasture. I did not want to see the lead rope cradled in her hands attached to an empty halter. I did not want to see the emptiness, the void, the quiet; but she kept coming as the memories raged across my consciousness.

I called out to her to go away. I could not take hearing what she had to say. Then I saw she was carrying something else in her hands, and as she walked, she was stroking it.

I begged her not to come close as she walked through the horses and up the stairs to stand before me. Her face was lined with grief, her eyes red and swollen with tears, her shoulders slumped forward with sadness, and in a very raspy and shaky voice, she asked me to hold out my hand. I shook my head no and wanted it all to go away, but she would not let it. Through the blur of tears and sounds of sobs, she leaned forward, took my hand, and dropped a long and beautiful braid of hair into my shaking palm. I clutched it firmly and noted its texture. I held it to my nose as the shock ran through my body. I pressed it to my eyes and wiped the tears with it.

"It's from Him," she said. "He wanted you to have a part of Him to love and to hold; He gave it to you." I sobbed as I held on to the braided tail. We both sobbed and rocked for what seemed like hours as the horses stood with their heads hanging over the rails of the little gazebo, gently nuzzling us.

"They need us," she said, "There is still much to do." And with those words, she gently opened my hand, took the braided tail hair, and went to each and every horse to let them smell it as she whispered into their ears, first Harley, then Pele, Bart and Apache. Each smelled the braid of their brother and heard her words. They stood with heads hanging as she came back to join me in the gazebo.

She wrapped her arms around me as Harley raised his head and called out to the heavens, Pele joined him followed by Bart, as Apache just stood and looked at us. When the horses stopped the call, the sound echoed and reverberated through the woods. Like a fleeting dream, we could hear it march off into the distance and when the ringing in our ears subsided, we listened. We, both horse and human alike, listened with all of our strength. For what I did not know: a reply, an answer, a sign? I had no idea.

As we all listened, we slowly became draped and covered in exactly what we were not listening for—the ambiance that we so very much struggled to avoid. The horses stood erect with their ears aimed forwards, we had stopped sobbing so we could hear what we heard. It sunk into all of us at the same time as the horses heard it at the same moment we did. We heard them sigh as we began to sob again. We had heard it; we all heard it loud and clear. There was no denying that it was the sound of silence, the resonance of emptiness, and the echo of tremendous loss. It was so very, very, very quiet.

EPILOGUE

And so, Ethan left us on December 4, 2007—my teacher, my friend, my mentor, and my guide. The voice of the herd had been silenced, and the quiet, to this day, is deafening.

Perhaps it is my fault. Maybe enough time has not passed. Perhaps I am not giving the other horses a chance. Whatever the reason, the whispers have ceased. Through the sorrow and loss, I selfishly crave and miss his presence. I have much growing to do.

But, from his loss, a new chapter has begun; another doorway has opened. Ethan's best friend, Harley, is blossoming. On a lark, we recently asked our vet to re-exam Harley's formerly injured knee. Years ago the prognosis was not good, as it had over-calcified, and our vet, at that time, feared that if we were to ride him and he over-extended his leg, it could result in serious injury for both Harley and his rider. So, for seven long years, Harley has been condemned to the confines of his pasture and never allowed to go out and explore the world as Ethan, Bart, Pele, and Apache had. He would scream when we would ride away and run like a fool as we departed.

But now, the vet said that his knee looked fine and there was absolutely no reason not to experience the outside world with Harley and set him free to explore the trails. So, as hard as it might be to believe, Harley immediately took to having someone on his back and walks along the trails with only a halter.

I can sit on Harley for hours and never go anywhere, just sit, and Harley is happy. He simply falls asleep. We are so deeply moved by his gentleness, manners, and loving disposition.

But what pains us, is to realize that it took Ethan's departure to open our eyes to the fact that Harley needed us and was fit to move on to the next level. Why we were not more observant earlier, I will never know, but sometimes, when I am sharing time with Harley, I swear that I can hear Ethan's nicker in the background. Sometimes, I feel that Ethan is near. Maybe, just maybe, there is hope.

You may be that hope. It is you who read these stories; it is you whom the horses have reached out to; and it is you who has contributed to Habitat for Horses, as a portion of the proceeds from the purchase of this book has been donated to HfH to continue to their efforts to help the horses.

The horses spoke of past abuse, of slaughter, and of injustice, If these issues speak to your heart and soul, then please visit www.habitatforhorses.org and become a part of the movement to stop the shipping of horses across our borders for slaughter, save the wild Mustangs from extinction, and educate your family and friends on the plight of the American Horse in general. There are a lot of dedicated people, and horses, out there who would love to call you a friend. Just take a second to reach out, and an entirely different world will become yours.

May The Force of the Horse be with you!

"Ethan, it is so!"

10217245R00169

Made in the USA
Charleston, SC
17 November 2011